GREAT MYSTERIES

Flying Saucers

OPPOSING VIEWPOINTS®

Look for these and other exciting *Great Mysteries: Opposing Viewpoints* books:

GREAT MYSTERIES

Flying Saucers

OPPOSING VIEWPOINTS®

by Don Nardo

Greenhaven Press, Inc.   P.O. Box 289009, San Diego, California 92198-9009

Library of Congress Cataloging-in-Publication Data

Nardo, Don, 1947–
    Flying Saucers : opposing viewpoints / by Don Nardo.
        p.   cm. — (Great mysteries)
    Includes bibliographical references and index.
    Summary: Discusses the debate over whether unidentified
flying objects really exist and how belief in them affects our culture.
    ISBN 1-56510-351-3   (alk. paper)
    1. Unidentified flying objects—Juvenile literature.
[1. Unidentified flying objects.]   I. Title.   II. Series: Great
mysteries (St. Paul, Minn.)
TL789.2.N37   1996
001.9'42—dc20   95-30344
                                      CIP
                                      AC

Contents

Introduction

This book is written for the curious—those who want to explore the mysteries that are everywhere. To be human is to be constantly surrounded by wonderment. How do birds fly? Are ghosts real? Can animals and people communicate? Was King Arthur a real person or a myth? Why did Amelia Earhart disappear? Did history really happen the way we think it did? Where did the world come from? Where is it going?

Great Mysteries: Opposing Viewpoints books are intended to offer the reader an opportunity to explore some of the many mysteries that both trouble and intrigue us. For the span of each book, we want the reader to feel that he or she is a scientist investigating the extinction of the dinosaurs, an archaeologist searching for clues to the origin of the great Egyptian pyramids, a psychic detective testing the existence of ESP.

One thing all mysteries have in common is that there is no ready answer. Often there are *many* answers but none on which even the majority of authorities agrees. *Great Mysteries: Opposing Viewpoints* books introduce the intriguing views of the experts, allowing the reader to participate in their explorations, their theories, and their disagreements as they try to explain the mysteries of our world.

But most readers won't want to stop here. These *Great Mysteries: Opposing Viewpoints* aim to stimulate the reader's curiosity. Although truth is often impossible to discover, the search is fascinating. It is up to the reader to examine the evidence, to decide whether the answer is there—or to explore further.

"Penetrating so many secrets, we cease to believe in the unknowable. But there it sits nevertheless, calmly licking its chops."

H. L. Mencken, American essayist

Prologue

The Flying Saucer Controversy

Shortly after midnight on August 23, 1954, a French businessman named Bernard Miserey arrived at his home in the village of Vernon, about forty miles northwest of Paris. After parking his car in the garage, Miserey claimed, he suddenly noticed something very strange. The whole village was illuminated by the glow of a pale light. Then, he looked up and saw that the glow was coming from a huge cigar-shaped object that was hovering, or floating almost motionless, in the sky. "I had been watching this amazing spectacle for a couple of minutes," Miserey later recalled,

> when suddenly from the bottom of the cigar came an object like a horizontal disk, which dropped at first in free fall, then slowed, and suddenly swayed and dived horizontally across the river toward me. For a very short time I could see the disk full-face; it was surrounded by a halo of brilliant light.

According to Miserey, in the following forty minutes or so four more disks emerged from the cigar and sped away. Then, the cigar itself faded and disappeared into the dark night.

Bernard Miserey was only one of thousands of people before and after him who claim to have seen

(Opposite page) This photo, supposedly of three flying saucers hovering over South Yorkshire, England, was taken in 1966. So far no saucer photo has been positively authenticated by scientists.

strange, unknown objects in the skies. Perhaps the most common name used to describe such objects is "flying saucers," although UFOs, which stands for "unidentified flying objects," is also popular. Sightings of flying saucers have been reported from nearly every country in the world and by people of all walks of life, from farmers and sheepherders to pilots and college professors. According to these witnesses, flying saucers come in a wide variety of shapes, sizes, and textures. Some are large, like the hovering cigar Miserey reported, while others are described as only one or two feet in diameter. Some are cigar-shaped, some round. Others are variously oval, flat, rodlike, lens-shaped, dark, bright, featureless, detailed, silver, red, blue, black, metallic, nonmetallic, rotating, gyrating, glowing, and/or pulsating. The actions attributed to flying saucers also vary considerably. Many reports describe them as hovering motionless, like Miserey's cigar. Others depict the saucers as zooming around the sky at tremendous speeds and performing maneuvers that

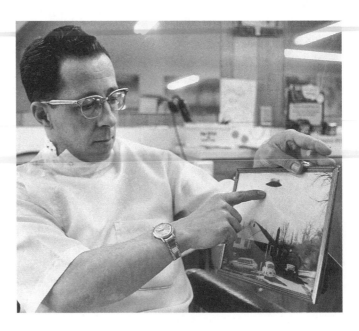

Ralph Ditter, a Zanesville, Ohio, barber and amateur astronomer, holds a picture of a flying saucer he claims to have taken in 1967.

would be impossible for earthly craft, such as making almost instant right-angled high-speed turns. In some reports, the saucers stay aloft, floating over towns or buzzing airplanes. In other sightings, however, the saucers land, leaving behind telltale marks or depressions in the dirt or grass.

In a number of more exotic reports, witnesses claim to have seen strange occupants exit the saucers. Some even claim that these occupants either invited them inside the objects or used force to carry them in. Typical was the case of Herbert Schirmer, a police officer in Ashland, Nebraska. On December 3, 1967, he claims, he saw a football-shaped object land, after which two occupants exited and approached him. "Are you the watchman of this town?" one occupant supposedly asked. "Yes, I am," Schirmer answered. According to Schirmer, the beings then took him inside their craft, where he found that "The crew leader had a very high forehead, and a very long nose; his eyes were sort of shrunken in, and they were round eyes like ours, except for their pupils [which] were sort of the form of a . . . cat's eye."

Believers

Assuming that Officer Schirmer was telling the truth and believed what he reported having seen, the important question becomes: What exactly *did* he see? This, of course, is another way of phrasing the central question of the entire, very puzzling flying saucer phenomenon. What are these bizarre objects? Those attempting to solve this great mystery fall, more or less, into two broad camps. The first group consists of people who can be termed "believers," that is, those who maintain not only that the saucers are real objects, but also that they are piloted craft. Most believers are convinced that these craft are "extraterrestrial," or from beyond the earth, and therefore that their occupants are alien beings from other planets.

"My own view is that there are no [UFO] cases that are simultaneously very reliable [reported independently by a large number of witnesses] and very exotic [not explicable in terms of reasonably postulated phenomena]."

American astronomer Carl Sagan, *The Cosmic Connection*

"I am convinced that . . . these [flying] disks are spaceships from another planet, operated by animate, intelligent beings."

Former navy commander Robert B. McLaughlin, in *True* magazine, March 1950

The most avid and vocal of the believers are sometimes referred to as flying saucer or UFO "enthusiasts," or as "ufologists." One of the first well-known enthusiasts was Ray Palmer, who became editor of the popular magazine *Amazing Stories* in 1938. Palmer helped formulate and define the believer theory, writing in the magazine's July 1946 issue, "If you don't think space ships visit the earth regularly . . . then . . . your editor's own files [of strange sightings] are something you should see. . . . And if you think responsible parties in world governments are ignorant of the fact of space ships visiting the earth, you just don't think the way we do." Later saucer enthusiasts echoed this theme. Typical was prolific author and former U.S. Marine Corps officer Donald E. Keyhoe, who stated in his 1973 book *Aliens from Space: The Real Story of Unidentified Flying Objects*, "During my long investigation of these strange objects I have seen many reports verified by AF [Air Force] Intelligence, detailed accounts by AF pilots, radar operators and other trained observers proving the UFOs are high-speed craft superior to anything built on earth."

Skeptics

On the opposite side in the flying saucer debate are those who are best described as "skeptics." Members of this group are skeptical, or highly in doubt, about the idea that the saucers are either piloted craft or of extraterrestrial origin. The skeptics say instead that the vast majority of flying saucer sightings can be explained in more conventional ways. According to this view, most sightings result from misidentification of natural phenomena, airplanes and other earthly craft, from deliberate hoaxes, or from the witnesses' imaginations. Stating the skeptics' case, scientist and science writer Philip J. Klass, who specializes in debunking, or exposing the falseness of, the believers' claims, wrote in his book *UFOs Explained*:

> "Like most people, I had grown up believing the earth was the center of everything. . . . Now, for the first time in my life, that belief was shaken. . . . We [are] faced with a race of beings at least two hundred years ahead of our civilization, perhaps thousands."
>
> Writer Donald E. Keyhoe, *The Flying Saucers Are Real*

> "There is . . . no reason so far to suppose that any UFO report can represent an extraterrestrial spaceship. An extraterrestrial spaceship is not inconceivable, to be sure, and one may show up tomorrow and will then have to be accepted. But at present there is no acceptable evidence for one."
>
> Science writer Isaac Asimov, *Extraterrestrial Civilizations*

The idea of wondrous space ships from a distant civilization really is a fairy story that is tailored to the adult mentality—a fairy story in which anyone can become a firsthand participant simply by keeping an alert eye peeled toward the skies.

The image in this photo is alleged to be of a flying saucer sighted over New Mexico in 1967.

According to skeptics like Klass, no sufficient, measurable evidence yet exists to support an otherworldly explanation for the saucers. As famed astronomer Carl Sagan put it, "There are no compelling cases of extraterrestrial visitation, despite all the claims about UFOs and ancient astronauts which sometimes make it seem that our planet is awash in uninvited guests. I wish it were otherwise."

Statements such as these typically punctuate the ongoing debate between the believers and the skeptics, an argument that constitutes the very core of the flying saucer controversy. That controversy is certain to continue well into the foreseeable future. This is because new sightings are reported regularly. These allegations, accompanied by analysis and commentary by believers and skeptics alike, add to the already vast body of saucer lore and literature. Indeed, with each passing year the mystery surrounding strange objects in the sky seems to deepen.

One

Visions of the Gods: Saucer Sightings in Past Ages

(Opposite page) A drawing depicts a swarm of strange black globes that many people said they saw floating over Basel, Switzerland, on August 7, 1566.

Both the term "flying saucer" and modern worldwide interest in the saucer mystery were born on June 24, 1947. On that day, thirty-two-year-old businessman and pilot Kenneth Arnold was flying his small plane over the Cascade Mountains in Washington State. Suddenly, he claimed, nine silvery, circular objects sped into view traveling at more than twelve hundred miles per hour. "I could see their outline quite plainly as they approached the mountain [Mt. Rainier]," Arnold later recalled. "They flew very close to the mountain-tops, flying like geese in a diagonal, chainlike line, as if they were linked together. They were flat like a pie-pan and so shiny that they reflected the sun like a mirror." Arnold also used another image to describe the objects to newspaper reporters: he said that they were like saucers being skipped over water. The news services apparently thought "flying saucers" sounded better than "flying pie-pans" and coined the term that stuck. In the months that followed, thousands of other people reported seeing strange objects in the skies. A major saucer "flap," or wave of sightings, the first of many, had begun.

But despite all the publicity and widespread interest it generated, the Arnold incident was far from

Businessman and pilot Kenneth Arnold displays his own drawing of one of the flying objects he claimed to have encountered near Mt. Rainier in Washington in 1947.

the earliest report of someone seeing an unknown flying object. In fact, human beings have seen strange, unidentified objects in the skies for thousands of years. Before the first modern saucer flap, these sightings generated only occasional public attention and had, for the most part, acceptable supernatural or psychological explanations. Some people assumed the sightings were religious in nature—visions of gods, angels, or other heavenly visitors. Another and similar common view was that strange objects in the sky were omens, heavenly signs that foretold something important. Many people, on the other hand, held that such sightings were delusions manufactured in the minds of mentally unbalanced persons.

However, with the advent of modern interest in saucers and the extraterrestrial hypothesis to explain them, people began to reexamine the older reports. Some believers see striking similarities between historical and modern descriptions of bizarre sky phenomena. Perhaps, they suggest, alien craft did not first arrive in the twentieth century, but have been periodically visiting the earth for many centuries.

Fire Circles and a Sound like Thunder

Perhaps the earliest prescientific record cited by believers as a description of extraterrestrial saucers is found in the *Annals of Thutmosis III*, an Egyptian papyrus, or scroll, attributed to the pharaoh named in the title. The scroll, dating from about 1450 B.C., tells of "fire circles" that appeared in the night sky, "a marvel never before known since the foundation of the land." According to this ancient document:

> The scribes of the House of Life [temple] found a circle of fire that was coming in the sky. . . . It had no head, and the breath of its mouth had a foul odor. . . . It had no voice. Now after some days had passed, these things became more numerous in the sky than ever. They shone more in the sky than the brightness of the heavens, and extended to the limits of the four supports of the heavens.

After witnessing these events, Thutmosis ordered the Egyptian priests to burn incense to appease the gods, who, he assumed, had sent the fire circles.

Other ancient references often cited as evidence of early flying saucers appear in India's two great religious epic poems—the *Mahabharata* and the *Ramayana*. The first, compiled in stages between the fifth century B.C. and fourth century A.D., contains the teachings of the Hindu god Krishna. The second, written in the third century B.C., chronicles the adventures of the god Rama. Both poems mention disklike flying machines called *vimanas*, which are described as having terrible destructive powers. The following excerpt from the *Mahabharata* depicts the destruction of the city of Varanasi by a *vimana* "discus," or flying disk:

> Varanasi burned, with all its princes and their followers, its inhabitants, horses, elephants, treasures and granaries, houses, palaces, and

markets. The whole of a city that was inaccessible to [defiant of] the gods was thus wrapped in flames by the discus . . . and was totally destroyed. The discus, then, with unmitigated [undiminished] wrath, and blazing fiercely . . . returned to the hand of Vishnu [the Preserver, one of the three main Hindu gods].

A number of saucer enthusiasts, including the popular Swiss writer Erich von Daniken, also cite passages from the Bible to support their belief in ancient extraterrestrial visitations. In the most often quoted passage, which is from the Book of Ezekiel, the prophet claims:

As I looked, behold, a stormy wind came out of the north, and a great cloud, with brightness round about it, and fire flashing forth continually, and in the midst of the fire, as it were gleaming bronze. And from the midst of it came the likeness of four living creatures. . . . Now as I looked at the living creatures, I saw a wheel upon the earth beside [them] . . . one for each of the four of them. . . . The four had the same likeness, their construction being as it were a wheel within a wheel. . . . When the living creatures went, the wheels went beside them; and when the living creatures rose from the earth, the wheels rose. . . . Over the heads of the living creatures there was the likeness of a firmament [hemisphere], shining like crystal. . . . And when they went, I heard the sound of their wings like the sound of many waters, like the thunder of the Almighty.

According to von Daniken and other believers, the "cloud" and "flashing fire" suggest the engine exhaust of some kind of piloted aircraft. The reference to "gleaming bronze" implies that the craft was metallic. Believers see the "wheel" and "wheel within a wheel" from which the occupants exited as evidence that the craft had a circular shape. The mention of multiple wheels may indicate that more than one airship was involved or that multiple landing craft came out of a larger ship. The "crystal firmament" clearly suggests a transparent dome through which some occupants could be seen. And the "sound like thunder," say believers, could have been the roar of the craft's engines.

Runways of the Gods?

The Ezekiel passage is just one piece of evidence cited by those who advocate the "ancient astronaut" hypothesis. According to this view, presented in considerable detail by von Daniken in *Chariots of the Gods?, The Gold of the Gods*, and other books, alien beings landed on earth in ancient times. These visitors interacted with humans, and even married them. They taught early societies how to build great monuments such as the Egyptian and Mayan pyramids, and when they finally departed, people remembered them as gods. Among his proofs, von Daniken cites numerous ancient paintings and carvings that appear to show beings with strange suits and helmets.

Von Daniken's ideas rest partly on his interpretation of the huge markings carved into the barren Nazca plateau in the South American country of Peru. In addition to numerous etchings of geometrical shapes and animals, there are groupings of long straight lines that look very much like the outlines of runways. Von Daniken claims that these markings are part of an early alien landing strip. According to archaeologists, these carvings were made between 400 B.C. and A.D. 900. What makes the carvings unusual is that because of their great size and the flatness of the plain, the pictures as a whole can be seen only from above. Since the Nazcas, the people who inhabited the area, had no airships, von Daniken argues, they must have intended that the carvings be viewed by the "visitors." "Seen from the air," von Daniken writes,

> the clear-cut impression that the 37-mile-long Plain of Nazca made on *me* was that of an

"I [find] that Ezekiel's spaceship has very credible dimensions and belongs to a stage of technology which modern man will not reach for some decades!"

NASA engineer Joseph F. Blumrich, quoted by writer Erich von Daniken in *The Gold of the Gods*

"Advocates of ancient astronauts [such as] Erich von Daniken . . . assert that there are numerous pieces of archaeological evidence that can be understood only by past contact with extraterrestrial civilizations. . . . But in every case the artifacts in question have plausible and much simpler explanations."

Carl Sagan, *Broca's Brain: Reflections on the Romance of Science*

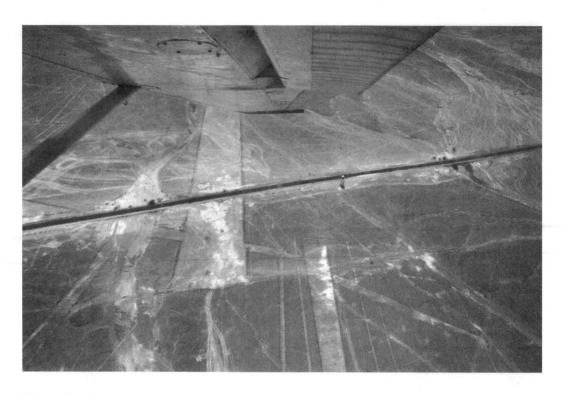

This aerial view shows part of the complex pattern of lines etched into the Nazca plateau in Peru.

airfield. In that case, what purpose did the lines at Nazca serve? According to my way of thinking, they could have been . . . built according to instructions from an aircraft. . . . What is wrong with the idea that the lines were laid out to say to the "gods": "Land here! Everything has been prepared as you ordered"?

Other Premodern Sightings

Some believers cite European historical records from the period in which the Nazca carvings were made to support their argument that extraterrestrials visited the earth. In the fourth century A.D., for instance, the Roman writer Julius Obsequens wrote his *Book of Prodigies*, a long list of omens witnessed by his countrymen. Among the events he reported were sightings of "round shields" and "burning globes" moving about in the skies above Rome.

Another sighting of mysterious flying shields occurred in about the year 900. According to a tract from the *Annales Laurissenses*, a series of annual chronicles of everyday life compiled by French monks, the objects appeared during the siege of a French town by the English Saxons:

> Now when the Saxons perceived things were not going in their favor, they began to erect scaffolding from which they could bravely storm the castle. But God is good as well as just. . . . Those watching outside in that place, of whom many still live to this very day, say they beheld the likeness of two large shields reddish in color in motion above the church, and when the pagans [non-Christians] who were outside saw this sign, they were at once thrown into confusion and, terrified with great fear, they began to flee from the castle.

In this case, God is mentioned as a possible source of the mysterious objects. The chroniclers *were* monks, after all, and it was only natural for them to attribute extraordinary happenings to the hand of God. In any case, in keeping with the straightforward narrative style of the chronicle, the excerpt seems less a religious allegory and more an honest attempt to record an event as it happened. Similar sightings of odd flying objects were recorded over the centuries that followed. What witnesses described variously as smoking cylinders, black spheres, fiery lights, and floating cigars appeared over Germany and Switzerland in the 1500s, Russia in the 1600s, and Mexico in the 1800s.

The Great Airship

Perhaps the most widely witnessed and sensational premodern series of sightings of an unknown flying object occurred in the United States between November 1896 and May 1897. Thousands of people in Alabama, Arkansas, Tennessee, Texas, Missouri, Colorado, California, and elsewhere claimed to have seen what became known as the "Great Airship." Exact descriptions varied, suggesting, for example, that some witnesses reported what they saw inaccurately or that more than one object was involved. Most described the airship as a huge cigar- or egg-shaped object that flew through the night sky. And almost everyone said that the airship had lights attached to it. A Wisconsin witness stated that "the white light . . . ahead and a red light at the rear made the affair look like a machine about fifty feet long and flying about 500 feet above the earth." Many people reported seeing the airship land. In some accounts, men climbed out of the ship, inspected and repaired the craft, and even spoke to astounded onlookers. In most of these cases, the occupants' language was unfamiliar.

Some later writers called the Great Airship extremely mysterious and impossible to explain in terms of human technology. The airship sightings occurred, after all, nearly six years before the Wright brothers made the first successful airplane flight at Kitty Hawk, North Carolina. In *The UFO Controversy in America*, David Michael Jacobs writes, "All evidence indicates that scientific knowledge about powered flight in 1896 and 1897 could not have led to the invention of airships with the characteristics witnesses described."

Fooled by the Unexplained

In response to theories about ancient, medieval, and other premodern alien visitations, skeptics generally argue that the stories and writings believers cite can be interpreted in other ways. Say skeptics, people in the past were much more easily disturbed, awed, and fooled by events they could not explain than are people today. This is because most past ages were prescientific. In such times, beliefs about natural phenomena that are now well understood by scientists were clouded by ignorance, fear, and superstition. Meteors and comets, exotic forms of

> "About sixty-five thousand years ago, extraordinary visitors came from another civilization in space . . . [and] decided to create a hybrid race, so that crossbreeding with humans after a few generations, that new race would be perfectly adapted to life on earth."
>
> Writer Maurice Chatelaine, *Our Ancestors Came from Outer Space*

> "Sexual love between a human being and an inhabitant of another planet ignores, in the most fundamental sense, the biological realities. . . . A viable offspring would not be possible. . . . Such crossings are about as reasonable as the mating of a man and a petunia."
>
> Carl Sagan, *The Cosmic Connection*

This illustration of the mysterious "Great Airship," sighted over many parts of the United States at the end of the last century, appeared in the *Chicago Times-Herald* on April 12, 1897.

lightning, and light distortions caused by atmospheric heat and dust are among the natural events that confused and alarmed premodern people.

For example, some skeptics say that the Thutmosis scroll, describing "fire circles" in the sky, could be based on sightings of a meteor swarm, a rare but awe-inspiring event. Astronomers explain that occasionally the earth is bombarded by a cloud of meteors, hunks of rock that travel through the solar system. Most are tiny, and friction causes them to burn up when they enter the upper atmosphere, creating the brilliant flashes of light commonly called "shooting stars." Larger and rarer meteoric chunks can and do make it all the way to the ground. They sometimes travel almost parallel to the earth's surface for minutes at a time, putting on impressive celestial light shows, before crashing.

Similarly, skeptics argue, a large meteor crash might be the inspiration for the account of the destruction of the city of Varanasi in the Indian epic. Because of its great speed, such a falling rock would not have had to be very large to do great damage. As one noted science writer, the late Isaac

A meteorite, the remains of a meteor that has reached the earth from outer space. Scientists say it is possible that some sightings of flying saucers are misidentifications of meteors and other celestial objects.

Asimov, explained in his book *A Choice of Catastrophes:*

> The largest known meteorite [the name given a meteor after it hits the earth] is still in the ground in Namibia in southwest Africa. It is estimated to weigh about 66 tons. . . . Even meteorites no larger than that could do considerable damage to property and kill hundreds, even thousands, of people, if they landed in a densely populated city area.

Skeptics are also reluctant to attribute the biblical passage quoted earlier to alien visitation. They point out that if taken literally as a description of a spaceship, the words of Ezekial are more suggestive of the crude rocket ships depicted in early science fiction stories than of sophisticated interplanetary craft. It is certainly difficult to believe that such advanced spaceships would utilize conventional, polluting, and noisy engines. Even in more modern depictions of flying saucers, the craft are almost always described as having no discernible exhaust and operating in silence.

Besides, says skeptic Ronald D. Story in his book *Guardians of the Universe?*, passages from religious works like the Bible and the *Mahabharata* should not be interpreted so literally. Story claims that von Daniken falsely "creates the illusion that the Bible is really just a straightforward account of spaceships landing and spacemen trotting all over the place." Instead, says Story, such passages are usually allegories, symbolic narratives intended to illustrate a moral idea or principle. These writings commonly appeared long after the incidents described were supposed to have occurred and may not represent memories of real events.

"Our Ancestors Were No Dummies"

Skeptics like Story also take issue with the ancient-astronaut thesis championed by von Daniken and others. In the skeptical view, the Nazca lines, like so much of von Daniken's cited evidence, can easily be explained without resorting to alien visitation. For example, the lines that seem to form runways might have served a mundane but important purpose for the natives. Long Island University professor Paul Kosok visited the Nazca plain in 1941 and discovered that one of the long lines points directly toward the sun on June 22, which marks the winter solstice, or first day of winter, in the Southern Hemisphere. Perhaps, then, some of the carvings were crude attempts at keeping a calendar. Another argument offered by skeptics against the runway idea is that flying saucers are supposed to be sophisticated craft that can land and take off vertically. If so, there would be no need for the kind of long runway required by twentieth-century airplanes.

Moreover, say skeptics, the idea that ancient humans could not have constructed large or sophisticated monuments without "outside" help is an insult to human intelligence and ingenuity. For instance, evidence showing how the Nazcas could have made the huge carvings on their own was uncovered on the plain by researchers in the 1970s and 1980s. Remnants of ropes, canvaslike material, and fire pits suggest that the Nazcas built primitive hot air balloons and sent them aloft using rising heat from bonfires. This would explain why the carvings appear to have been executed with help from airborne observers. "Our ancestors were no dummies," states Carl Sagan in his book *Broca's Brain*. "They may have lacked high technology, but they were as smart as we, and they sometimes combined dedication, intelligence and hard work to produce results that impress even us."

Human ingenuity, skeptics suggest, may also have been behind the sightings of the mysterious Great Airship in the late 1800s. Well-known skeptics like Philip Klass point out that early versions of dirigibles, commonly called blimps, were in the experimental stage even before 1896. The first dirigibles were huge, hydrogen-gas-filled bags that carried passengers in small compartments on their undersides. According to Klass:

> Primitive powered airships of this type had been developed in Europe. For example, in 1884, a French airship [built by Charles Renard and

One of the many large figures representing animals that were carved into Peru's Nazca plateau more than one thousand years ago.

A. C. Krebs] measuring 165 feet long had managed to fly a five-mile closed course at an average speed of 13 mph. . . . Numerous American inventors were trying to develop "flying machines," and on May 6, 1896, only a few months before the rash of "mysterious airship" reports, Samuel P. Langley had successfully flown a twenty-six-pound model airplane, a feat that made headlines.

Klass maintains that the reported cigarlike shape of the Great Airship and the numerous reports of ordinary-looking humans exiting the craft are more suggestive of a dirigible than an alien spaceship. Perhaps the occupants spoke in unfamiliar tongues because the most advanced experiments on heavier-than-air flying craft were ongoing in France and Germany. Did foreign inventors make unauthorized and unpublicized experimental dirigible flights over the United States? This possibility remains unproven. But given the nature of the accounts, say skeptics, it is much more credible than the idea that the airship was extraterrestrial.

A Fantastic Idea

It is interesting to note that few reporters or writers at the time of the sightings suggested that the Great Airship was of alien origins. Maybe this was because the vast majority of people still did not believe that flying machines were remotely possible. Even after the first officially recorded dirigible flights in Germany in 1900, most people still saw the idea of heavier-than-air machines' getting off the ground as fantastic. In 1901, just two years before the Wright brothers' feat, a *New York Times* editorial predicted that it would take up to ten million years for humans to conquer the air! Perhaps it is not surprising, therefore, that widespread public interest in and acceptance of the idea of alien saucers would come later, with the advent of rockets, atom bombs, and other examples of advanced technology.

"Were the pyramids built by architects from . . . some extraterrestrial source? Is the Great Pyramid of Cheops the physical embodiment of a lost science of vast antiquity and unsurpassed knowledge?"

Writer Brad Steiger, *Worlds Before Our Own*

"It is a mistake to believe that the ancients were not every bit as intelligent as we. Their technology was more primitive, but their brains were not."

Isaac Asimov, *Extraterrestrial Civilizations*

Two

Bright Lights and Bogies: The Modern Saucer Era Is Born

Before the 1940s, the idea of alien beings visiting the earth was a fascinating but largely fanciful one that remained mainly in the realm of popular fiction. Many people enjoyed but did not take seriously books such as H. G. Wells's *War of the Worlds*, which depicts a Martian invasion of the earth. The kinds of advanced technology described seemed much too improbable, if not impossible. Thus, people usually continued to explain away strange flying objects in fairly mundane ways. For example, when World War II pilots reported seeing "foo fighters," luminous colored lights hovering near their planes, most military personnel assumed that these phantoms were secret enemy devices.

But this situation changed with the advent of high-flying rockets and especially destructive atomic bombs at the end of that same world war. Suddenly, it seemed possible to many people that humans might, at least within a few centuries, develop the technology needed to fly between planets. And if humans could do so, could not aliens, who might be centuries ahead of us, already have done so? Although the concept of extraterrestrial craft had rarely been discussed in a serious manner, reputable sources now increasingly considered the idea.

(Opposite page) A trio of what appear to be strange flying craft hover over the Italian countryside in this 1960 photo.

During World War II, U.S. bomber pilots reported seeing glowing objects zooming alongside their planes. Dubbed "foo fighters," these strange but harmless objects were never explained.

On July 6, 1947, for instance, the highly respected *New York Times* published a list of possible explanations for strange objects seen in the skies. Besides natural and human-made phenomena, the article stated, "They may be visitants [visitors] from another planet launched from spaceships anchored above the stratosphere [upper atmosphere]."

The 1947 Arnold incident, therefore, came at a time when public perceptions about unknown objects in the skies were changing. As Richard Williams explains in *UFO: The Continuing Enigma:*

> After Arnold's "flying saucer" sighting, a small but growing percentage of the population began to believe in the physical reality of nuts-and-bolts craft from other planets visiting the earth. UFOs were finally here to stay.

Indeed, Arnold's sighting launched the modern "saucer era," a relentless onslaught of saucer reports that has continued, virtually uninterrupted, to the present.

Close Encounters

The nature of the saucer reports has varied widely. In some, witnesses described bizarre flying lights or craft hovering or zooming around, while in others the craft actually have landed and left burn marks or depressions on the ground. In still others, witnesses claimed to have seen or encountered the occupants of the craft. For many years there seemed to be no clear and easy way to categorize and classify the various reports.

Eventually, astronomer and well-known saucer investigator J. Allen Hynek offered the now familiar "close encounters" system. In his book *The UFO Experience: A Scientific Inquiry*, Hynek wrote:

> There appear to be three natural subdivisions [of most saucer reports], which we can call, respectively, *Close Encounters of the First, Second, and Third Kinds. . . . Close Encounters of the First Kind:* this category is the simple Close Encounter, in which the reported UFO is seen at close range but there is no interaction with the environment. . . . *Encounters of the Second Kind:* these are similar to the First Kind except that physical effects on both animate [living] and inanimate [nonliving] material are noted. Vegetation [for instance] is often reported as having been pressed down, burned, or scorched. . . . *Close Encounters of the Third Kind:* in these cases the presence of "occupants" in or about the UFO is reported.

It is easy to fit the "classic," or most famous or baffling, cases of the early saucer era into Hynek's system. The Arnold sighting, for example, would be considered a close encounter of the first kind, since the nine disks the pilot saw did not seem to affect the environment and no occupants were reported.

"A careful scrutiny of the sky revealed Venus, and it could be that . . . Mantell did actually give chase to [the image of] the planet, even though whatever objects had been the source of the excitement elsewhere had disappeared."

Scientist J. Allen Hynek, quoted by Edward J. Ruppelt in *The Report on Unidentified Flying Objects*

"The most probable explanation is that Captain Mantell did, indeed, confront a skyhook [balloon] . . . launched from Camp Ripley, Minnesota, early on the morning that Captain Mantell was killed."

David R. Saunders and R. Roger Harkins, *UFOS? Yes!: Where the Condon Committee Went Wrong*

The Arnold incident is seen as a classic case partly because it was the first important sighting, the one that launched an era. Moreover it could not easily be explained away as a misidentification of a natural phenomenon. Arnold claimed he was sure that the disks were not birds flying in formation or reflections of the sun's image on distant clouds.

The Mysterious Mantell Incident

A number of other sightings in the early years of the flying saucer era are now considered classics. These also received a great deal of publicity and seemed, at least at first, to be unexplainable in natural terms and therefore strong evidence of alien craft. The first great post-Arnold classic occurred on January 7, 1948. Four Air National Guard F-51 fighter planes, one of them piloted by Captain Thomas F. Mantell, were nearing Godman Air Force Base in Kentucky on a standard training flight. At about 1:20 P.M., the Kentucky State Police reported seeing a large circular object floating through the sky. When this report reached the Godman base, Mantell and others were asked by their superiors to investigate.

At 2:45, Mantell radioed that he could see the object. As his plane climbed ever higher in pursuit, he reported, "The object is directly ahead of and above me now, moving at about half my speed. It appears to be a metallic object or possibly [a] reflection of the sun from a metallic object, and it is of tremendous size." A few seconds later, Mantell radioed, "I'm still climbing, the object is above and ahead of me moving at about my speed or faster. I'm trying to close in for a better look."

Not long after that, the Godman tower lost contact with Mantell and his plane crashed near Franklin, Kentucky. When air force personnel reached the scene, they found his lifeless body still lodged in the cockpit. The immediate reaction of both press and public was that Mantell had encountered a saucer similar to those seen by Arnold. The next day the *Louisville Courier* carried the headline, "F-51 and Capt. Mantell Destroyed Chasing Flying Saucer," and similar headlines spread to front pages nationwide. Recalls aerospace historian Curtis Peebles:

> With the headlines came wild rumors—the flying saucer was a Soviet missile; it was a spacecraft that knocked down the F-51 when it got too close; Captain Mantell's body was riddled with bullets; the body was missing; the plane had completely disintegrated in the air; the wreckage was radioactive.

In the following months and years, those who believed the saucer explanation used one or more of these rumors to support their position.

A Secret Skyhook?

Yet, extensive investigations failed to produce any convincing evidence to substantiate any of the rumors. Captain Mantell's body was neither missing nor bullet-riddled, and the plane was not radioactive. Experts concluded that the pilot, who had not been equipped with breathing gear, had passed out from lack of oxygen at an altitude of twenty-five thousand feet, whereupon the plane had spun out of control and crashed. No conclusive identification has ever been made for the object Mantell was chasing. But skeptical investigators have offered a number of theories. Scientist and saucer skeptic Donald H. Menzel, for example, speculated in his 1953 book, *Flying Saucers*, that Mantell and the other witnesses had seen a "mock sun," a reflection of the sun's image on atmospheric ice crystals.

Perhaps the most convincing scientific explanation for the Mantell case was proposed in 1952 by an air force captain, Edward J. Ruppelt. On January 22, 1948, only two weeks after Mantell's mysterious death, the air force had set up Project Sign, an operation designed to review and offer explanations

Captain Thomas F. Mantell died chasing an unknown object that some people suggested might have been an alien craft. The Mantell incident became one of the flying saucer "classics."

U.S. Air Force officers Captain Edward J. Ruppelt (left) and Major General John Samford. Ruppelt served as the first director of the air force's Project Blue Book.

for the increasing number of saucer sightings. In February 1949 the operation's name was changed to Project Grudge. Ruppelt became director of the operation shortly before it underwent another name change—this time to Project Blue Book—in March 1952. Project Sign investigators had concluded that Mantell had chased a distorted image of the planet Venus. But Ruppelt was doubtful. No matter how distorted by the upper atmosphere, he reasoned, Venus's image would remain little more than a point of light. Yet all the witnesses had reported seeing an object with a definite and very large visible diameter.

Ruppelt reopened the case and discovered that on the very day of the Mantell incident the U.S. Navy had been testing a secret "Skyhook" high-altitude balloon that air force officials knew nothing about. The balloon had been launched from a base in Minnesota early that morning. Studies of weather charts for that day showed that the Skyhook could have drifted over Kentucky. Furthermore, a local astronomer had seen the reported object late in the afternoon, viewed it with binoculars, and described it as "a pear-shaped balloon with cables and a basket attached." On the basis of these findings, Ruppelt decided that Mantell had died pursuing a large shiny balloon that had been whipped along at high speeds by currents in the upper atmosphere. Many believers remained unconvinced, however. They pointed out that while the astronomer seems to have spotted the balloon in question, Mantell may well have been chasing a completely different object.

The Fort Monmouth and Washington, D.C., Sightings

Believers also pointed out that a number of other widely publicized sightings had mysterious features and were worthy of continued investigation. Among these were a series of sightings that occurred over Fort Monmouth, New Jersey, on September 10 and 11, 1951. The occupants of a T-33 jet training plane flying at twenty thousand feet reported seeing a dull, silvery disk about forty feet in diameter flying near their craft. Ground-based radar operators tracked the object, which seemed to rise straight up and then perform various aerial maneuvers. Investigators who studied the case concluded that the radar operators had mistakenly tracked a normal airplane and also a weather balloon and that the witnesses in the T-33 had seen one or more balloons. However, some later investigators and writers insisted that the pilot of the T-33 was sure he had not seen a balloon and that at least part of the incident remained unexplained.

Another classic case that remains unexplained happened during the night of July 19-20 and again on July 26, 1952, in the skies over Washington, D.C. Radar operators at Washington National Airport tracked eight or more objects, which they were sure were not conventional airplanes, zooming around the U.S. capital's restricted airspace. Airline pilots flying in the area also saw strange lights either hovering in the air or moving rapidly through the night sky. When radar operators suggested that the pilots move in for a closer look, the lights careened away. The pilot of an F-94 interceptor jet tried to chase four of the lights on July 26 and made the following report:

> I tried to make contact with the bogies [targets] below 1,000 feet. . . . I saw several bright lights.

This photo, taken on July 19, 1952, shows three airway operations specialists watching a radar scope at Washington National Airport, a facility that figured prominently in that year's huge flying saucer "flap."

I was at my maximum speed, but even then I had
no closing speed. I ceased chasing them because
I saw no chance of overtaking them.

The official verdict by air force investigators on the Washington, D.C., sightings was that the radar images and sky lights had been mirages caused by unusual weather phenomena. But some believers disagreed. Donald Keyhoe later interviewed two of the Washington National Airport radar operators, who told him that they were convinced that "unknown visitors" heard their instructions to the airline pilots. This seemed to explain why the "spacecraft" sped away from the airliners only seconds after each instruction was given.

Electrical Fields Dampened

The Washington, D.C., sightings turned out to be part of a huge saucer flap that continued during the remaining months of 1952. In all, Project Blue Book received 1,501 reports in that year, of which 303 remained officially unidentified after investigation and study. Similar but somewhat smaller waves of sightings occurred in the years that followed. In 1957, for example, 1,006 sightings were reported, 14 of which were classified as "unknowns." Most air force investigators and civilian scientists assumed that the cases marked unidentified or unknown had logical, mundane causes that could not be explained because there was not enough evidence to work with.

By contrast, believers held that many of the unknowns might well be alien craft. By this time, J. Allen Hynek had been joined by a few other qualified and respected scientists who deemed the extraterrestrial hypothesis for the saucers worthy of more serious investigation. Some of these scientists criticized the air force for failing even to investigate many of the sightings. Dr. James E. McDonald, then a physicist at the University of Arizona, also accused Blue Book representatives of doing a sloppy

Lieutenant Colonel Hector Quintanilla, director of Project Blue Book in the early 1960s, examines evidence connected with a purported flying saucer sighting.

job of studying those important cases they *did* investigate.

Another classic saucer incident, which occurred in 1957 near Levelland, Texas, was a case in point. Historian and UFO researcher David Michael Jacobs summarizes the Levelland sightings in his book T*he UFO Controversy in America:*

The sightings began at 11:00 P.M. on the night of November 2 and ended at 2:00 A.M. on the morning of November 3. Two witnesses, driving just north of Levelland, saw a glowing, yellow and white, torpedo-shaped object flying toward them. As the object flew over the automobile, the car's motor and lights failed. The two witnesses left their car to view the object, and it came so close to them that they experienced "quite some heat," which forced them to "hit the ground." As the object left the area, the driver could start the car again and turn the lights on. One hour later, at midnight, a witness driving four miles east of Levelland came upon a brilliantly glowing, egg-shaped object resting in the middle of the road. As the witness approached the object . . . the car's engine and lights failed.

In the next two hours, several other people in the area reported run-ins with the bizarre object and said that their car engines had temporarily stalled. In fact, there were twelve unrelated witnesses in all, and the reports were widely spaced.

Investigation Criticized

McDonald and others later criticized Project Blue Book for the way it handled the case. The entire investigation, they charged, consisted of a single man who spent about a day in Levelland and did not even interview nine of the witnesses. The investigator blamed the stalled engines on "wet electrical circuits" due to stormy weather on the night of the incident. Yet all the witnesses insisted that no storm had occurred and that their engines were never wet. Many believers, including Donald Keyhoe, joined McDonald in chiding the air force for its lax approach to the case.

The Levelland sightings also received a great deal of publicity because of the eerie nature of the events described. The "heat" felt by some witnesses, along with the stalled engines, were signs of the object's interacting with the immediate environment, which made the incident a close encounter of the second kind. This was the first time that flying saucers were reported to have stopped cars dead in the road. It would not be the last. Thereafter, stalled auto engines became a common element of many

"Weather phenomenon of electrical nature, generally classified as 'Ball Lightning' or 'St. Elmo's Fire,' caused by stormy conditions in the area, including mist, rain, thunderstorms and lightning."

Official U.S. Air Force explanation for the Levelland saucer sightings

"I think it's a space craft from some of the neighboring planets."

NICAP investigator of the Levelland sightings

"It appeared to go in a straight line and at [the] same height—possibly 10 to 15 feet from the ground. . . . [The] object was traveling very fast. It seemed to rise up, and take off immediately across country."

Witness Lonnie Zamora on the Socorro sighting

"If a spaceship from distant worlds just happened to land outside [Socorro, NM] a town that was sorely in need of a tourist attraction . . . the officials of that town should not be blamed for promptly acting to exploit their good fortune."

Saucer skeptic and writer Philip J. Klass, *UFOs Explained*

saucer reports and believers cited the "magnetic power" to dampen electrical fields as proof that the saucers were machines with highly sophisticated technology. In contrast, skeptics asked why no cars had stalled in the thousands of previously reported saucer encounters? It was more likely, they said, that later witnesses incorporated the detail of failed engines into their own reports after the Levelland case had made that detail part of the growing saucer "mythology."

Reliable Witnesses?

Skeptics have used cases like the Levelland incident to call attention to the reliability, or rather the lack thereof, of many saucer witnesses. According to this view, most of the Levelland witnesses were not trained observers and so could easily have misinterpreted natural phenomena. Usually, skeptics define a trained observer as a scientist, airplane pilot, military intelligence officer, police officer, or some other person whose job involves collecting and interpreting factual evidence. Yet even reports by such reliable witnesses should not automatically be accepted, say skeptics. After all, even experts can make mistakes. And of course, like anyone else, trained observers can lie. The possibility that self-described witnesses might purposely stage a saucer hoax, for publicity or some other reason, has always been recognized by believers and skeptics alike.

One of the most famous early sightings generated a controversy about both the witness's reliability and the possibility of a hoax. This was the 1964 incident in Socorro, New Mexico. On April 24 of that year patrolman Lonnie Zamora reported that he had seen an "egg-shaped vehicle" that had apparently landed in a rural area outside Socorro. Two figures, each about four feet tall and clad in white, stood beside the craft. When Zamora approached, the vehicle shot out a burst of flames and disappeared into the sky. Upon examining the landing site, the officer found burned vegetation and deep depressions left in the dirt by the "landing pads."

J. Allen Hynek himself investigated the incident and later stated, "Zamora, although not overly bright or articulate, is basically sincere, honest, and reliable. He would not be capable of contriving a complex hoax, nor would his temperament indicate that he would have the slightest interest in such." Another investigator, representing the National Investigations Committee on Aerial Phenomena, or NICAP, a well-organized group of saucer believers, agreed with Hynek. After inspecting the site and interviewing Zamora, the NICAP investigator published his conclusions in the July/August 1964 issue of the popular saucer magazine *The UFO Investigator.* "Intensive on-the-spot investigations by NICAP and the Air Force," the article reported, "have resulted in one basic agreement: That the object seen

Lonnie Zamora, who made the famous Socorro sighting, watches as air force investigators employ a Geiger counter to scan a bush for signs of radiation. The bush was supposedly scorched by the exhaust from the flying saucer Zamora encountered.

by a highly reliable witness cannot be explained as any known device or phenomenon."

One person who did *not* agree with Hynek and NICAP was skeptic Philip Klass. After conducting his own investigation of the Socorro case, Klass found several irregularities in Zamora's story. When Klass measured the depths of and distances between the prints supposedly left by the landing pads, he found that such pads would have to have been of unequal lengths and angles. This, said Klass, would have made the craft too unstable to stand upright on the ground. Klass also interviewed a man named Felix Phillips who lived only a thousand feet from the landing site. Phillips swore that his windows were wide open at the time of the incident and he heard nothing out of the ordinary. Zamora, however, had testified that the craft had made a deafening roar at a distance of over four thousand feet. In addition, Klass discovered that the town later planned to use the site as a tourist attraction. Based on these and other findings, he called the Socorro incident a hoax designed to stimulate tourism for the town.

A Classic Unknown

Not everyone agreed with Klass, of course, so the Socorro case is still considered a classic unknown. As Richard Williams puts it:

> Despite Klass's objections, the Socorro incident remains one of the most convincing UFO sightings ever recorded. . . . So far no one has been able to explain away the object Zamora saw or to prove conclusively that he was either in league with hoaxers, or their victim.

The Socorro incident was also important because it was one of the earlier versions of what Hynek called close encounters of the third kind, that is, cases involving saucer occupants. One major difference between this and most of the previous cases involving alien beings was that Zamora claimed only to have viewed the saucer occupants from a distance. He

GULF BREEZE

had not actually talked to or interacted with them. On the other hand, a small number of people claimed that they *had* made contact with aliens and as a result became known as the "contactees." These bold and outspoken individuals constituted, and still constitute, one of the most colorful and controversial elements of the flying saucer phenomenon.

Scientist and noted flying saucer debunker Philip Klass attends a conference on UFOs.

Three

Saving Humanity from Its Darker Self: The Contactees

The Arnold, Mantell, Washington, D.C., Socorro, and other classic incidents of the early modern saucer era vaulted the idea of intelligently controlled flying saucers into the world spotlight. Reports, discussions, and debates about the saucer phenomenon flooded newspapers, bookstores, and the radio and television airwaves. Much of this saucer "literature" consisted of the classics and reports similar to them, which mainly involved close encounters of the first and second kinds. Such reports stimulated a healthy, although at times angry, debate between believers and skeptics. On the believers' side were writers like Donald Keyhoe and well-known saucer groups, most notably NICAP, of which Keyhoe served for many years as director. On the skeptics' side were most air force investigators and also many civilian scientists and writers, including Philip Klass and Donald Menzel.

However, another important and highly publicized segment of the early saucer literature seemed to fall outside the primary saucer debate. This literature consisted of reports and stories that frustrated and irritated not only skeptics, but many believers as well. The controversial stories were those of the contactees, people who claimed personal contact,

(Opposite page) Physicist and UFO lecturer Stanton Friedman holds a photo of a sculpture made under hypnosis by a New Hampshire man. The man claimed that the being the sculpture depicts took him aboard a flying saucer in 1971.

communication, and interaction with alien beings. Various contactees continue to make such claims today. But they achieved a much higher level of public popularity and acceptance in the 1950s and 1960s, now seen as the classic "contactee era." Characterizing the classic contactees, David Jacobs writes:

> They did not report their "experiences" to a reputable investigatory agency. Instead, they publicized them by writing books and articles, presenting lectures, and appearing on radio and television shows. Indeed, the contactees had no fear of ridicule [as many other saucer witnesses did] and eagerly sought publicity. They often organized special flying saucer clubs based on their experiences and used the clubs to help publicize their stories. Also, their "experiences" often differed markedly from all other UFO observers, in that some contactees claimed to have taken a ride in a flying saucer and described the ride and the planets they visited in great detail. Moreover, most contactees reported that space people had charged them with a mission, which, they said, was why they had to seek publicity.

The Tall Stranger in the Desert

The first, most famous, and most widely accepted contactee was George Adamski. Born in Poland in 1891, he immigrated to the United States in 1913 and over the years held jobs ranging from cavalry soldier and maintenance worker to concrete contractor and hamburger cook. He and his wife were running a hamburger stand in southern California not far from Palomar Mountain, site of what was then the world's largest telescope, when the prelude to his first alien contact began. In his later writings, Adamski claimed that on October 9, 1946, he saw a large, dark object hovering in the night sky. Then, in August 1947 Adamski saw 184 flying saucers pass over Palomar Mountain. He became convinced not only that these craft were pi-

George Adamski, the hamburger cook who became internationally famous after claiming he made personal contact with beings from other worlds.

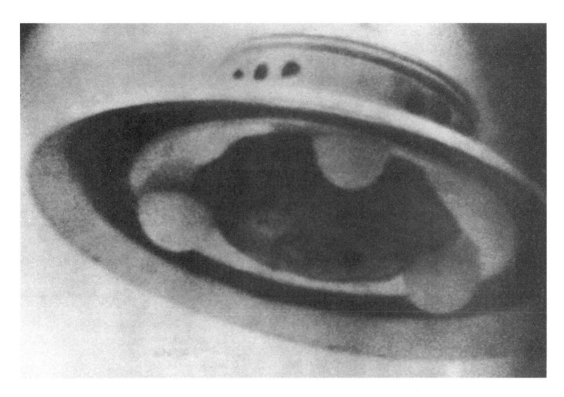

loted, but also that they sought eventual personal contact with him.

Eventually, Adamski wrote, on November 20, 1952, while driving with some friends in the nearby desert, he saw "a gigantic cigar-shaped silvery ship." Realizing his "time" had come, he exclaimed, "Someone get me down the road—quick! That ship has come looking for me and I don't want to keep them waiting!" When the car stopped, Adamski jumped out and ran off by himself. Soon, he said, he came upon a strange man, tall with shoulder-length hair, standing in a deserted ravine. According to Adamski, the stranger

> was round faced with an extremely high forehead; large, but calm, grey-green eyes, slightly aslant at the outer corners; with slightly higher cheekbones than an Occidental [white person], but not so high as an [American] Indian

One of Adamski's own photos of the flying saucer in which he allegedly rode. Investigators later showed that the object in the photo was human-made out of parts from a chicken brooder and other mechanical devices.

"We on earth really know very little about [the] Creator. . . . Our understanding is shallow. Theirs [the space brothers'] is much broader, and they adhere to the Laws of the Creator instead of laws of materialism as earth men do."

Self-described contactee George Adamski, quoted by Desmond Leslie in *Flying Saucers Have Landed*

"I do believe most definitely that Adamski's narrative contains enough flaws to place in very serious doubt both his veracity [honesty] and his sincerity."

Writer James W. Moseley, *Saucer News*, October 1957

or an Oriental [Asian]; a finely chiseled nose, not conspicuously large; and an average size mouth with beautiful white teeth that shone when he smiled or spoke.

Using both spoken words and "mental telepathy," Adamski communicated with the stranger and learned that his name was Orthon. A native of the planet Venus, Orthon had traveled to earth in a spaceship because his race was concerned about humanity's recent development of atomic weapons. These weapons, the Venusian warned, might destroy all life on earth and also contaminate outer space with dangerous radiation. Spacecraft from many planets and stars were visiting earth, Orthon told Adamski, but the occupants would not attempt public landings because fearful earthlings would surely "tear them to pieces."

Alien Cities on the Moon

Adamski wrote a sixty-page account of his contact with Orthon, and British writer Desmond Leslie included the tract in his own 1953 book, *Flying Saucers Have Landed*. Through this exposure, Adamski gained much publicity. He began to give lectures about his experience and eventually garnered tens of thousands of devoted followers in the United States and other countries. In 1955 he published his first full-length book, *Inside the Space Ships*, which enjoyed brisk sales. In the book, Adamski described new contacts with aliens, including his voyages in craft originating from Mars, Jupiter, and other planets, and conversations with an alien elder philosopher known as "the Master." Adamski also claimed to have seen forests, lakes, and alien cities on the far side of the moon, which at the time had not yet been seen or photographed by humans. In his third book, *Flying Saucers Farewell*, published in 1961, Adamski described his "mission" in the following way:

The knowledge shared by our space brothers must now be put to work. I have been advised to proceed in two fields that are vital to our progress—space philosophy and technology—which, we will learn, are inseparable in establishing a peaceful, productive society.

Humanity's "Only Hope"

George Adamski died in 1965 without having fulfilled his mission. But the contactee phenomenon that his report initiated lived on in his writings and in the stories, lectures, and books of others who claimed to be contactees. One of the earliest and most famous of these individuals was Truman Bethurum, a maintenance mechanic. In his 1954 book, *Aboard a Flying Saucer*, he described being led into a spaceship by ten "little men." Inside the ship, he

The provocative cover of Truman Bethurum's equally provocative 1954 book, in which he detailed his claim to have ridden in a flying saucer.

met the female captain, Aura Rhanes, who was "tops in shapeliness and beauty." Rhanes supposedly told Bethurum that she was from the planet Clarion, which was not visible to humans because it was located "behind the sun." The Clarionites, she said, were visiting earth out of concern for the "considerable confusion" that humanity's nuclear weapons might bring to other planets. Thereafter, Bethurum advocated that humans abolish such weapons in order to make the earth more like Clarion, a world unburdened by disease, war, and other earthly ills.

The year 1954 also witnessed the emergence of another contactee who gained a popular following over the years. He was Daniel Fry, a technician at an aeronautics company in New Mexico. Fry published *The White Sands Incident*, in which he claimed an alien being named A-lan invited him aboard a saucer for a ride to New York City and back. Later, Fry wrote another book, titled *A-lan's Message to Men of Earth*. According to A-lan, humanity's physical sciences, especially its weaponry, had developed faster than its religious and social morality. The "space brothers" had come to help foster the "understanding" among earth's peoples that was humanity's "only hope."

Aliens with a Mission

Another popular contactee, Los Angeles aircraft worker Orfeo Angelucci, told of his bizarre experiences in his 1955 book, *The Secret of the Saucers*. Like most other contactees, he claimed to have taken rides in flying saucers piloted by "space brothers." And like other contactee stories, this one depicted the aliens as arriving on earth to help save humanity from its darker self. Angelucci wrote:

> "For all its apparent beauty, earth is a purgatorial world [one suffering damnation for its sins]. . . . Hate, selfishness, and cruelty rise from many parts of it like a dark mist. . . . Your teacher has told you, God is love, and in those

Famous contactee George Van Tassel (left) in a TV appearance with television commentator Long John Nebel. Van Tassel claimed he used mental telepathy to communicate with aliens.

simple words may be found the secrets of all the mysteries of earth and the worlds beyond.

Although the stories told by Adamski, Bethurum, Fry, and Angelucci were very similar, the contactee phenomenon exhibited some variations. Not all the contactees were Americans, for instance. In the late 1950s a British citizen named James Cooke attracted a widespread following after claiming contact with aliens. After being invited into a saucer equipped with "dazzling lights," he recalled, he met several humanoids, or beings with human form, who told him they had come to help humanity. Other popular contactees differed in their method of contact. California aircraft mechanic George Van Tassel, for example, said that he communicated with aliens strictly through mental telepathy and did not meet them face-to-face. Van Tassel organized several conventions and meetings during the 1950s, 1960s, and 1970s that drew saucer believers from many states.

The "Lunatic Fringe"

The impact of the contactees on the flying saucer phenomenon and public perceptions of it was and remains enormous. In the first place, many of their books were immensely popular both in the United States and abroad and went into repeated printings over the years. Second, through giving lectures, staging conventions, and forming saucer clubs, the contactees established widespread followings. Van Tassel's conventions alone often attracted crowds of more than 5,000 people. According to Curtis Peebles:

> The conventions and flying saucer clubs created a network. This network gave believers an opportunity to meet other believers and exchange ideas, rumors, and reports. . . . The clubs held meetings and conventions, published newsletters, and sought new members/converts. They also gave publicity to the contactees by sponsoring public appearances. Through this network, the scattered believers were linked, becoming more than the sum of their parts. The contactees also used television and radio to spread their "message." This gave the contactees audiences of hundreds of thousands, or even millions.

Many believers eagerly accepted the contactees' accounts and expressed their happiness about the message of hope for humanity embodied in these stories. But not all the believers were so happy about the contactees. Many flying saucer investigators and writers bemoaned the huge public impact of the contactees as being much more negative than positive. Donald Keyhoe, for example, felt strongly that the contactees were liars and hoaxers that hurt the cause of serious saucer research. As David Jacobs puts it:

> The UFO phenomenon had always encountered ridicule, such that many reputable individuals were afraid to report sightings and scientists refused to view the subject seriously. Indeed, ridicule was probably the most decisive factor that prevented professional people and [a large

portion of] the public from treating the subject seriously.

Fearing that any serious debate about flying saucers would be killed by what he saw as the contactees' outrageous claims, Keyhoe refused to associate with these people or attend meetings at which they were guests. Through his efforts, NICAP and other investigatory believer groups treated the contactees in a hostile manner, calling them the "lunatic fringe" of the saucer phenomenon. But these efforts were not entirely successful. Indeed, says Jacobs:

> The contactees' emergence and their popularity and publicity succeeded in entrenching even deeper the ridicule factor in the public imagination. From the mid-1950s to 1972,

people with little knowledge of the phenomenon constantly confused the "lunatic fringe" with serious UFO investigators and researchers.

A New Religion?

Saucer skeptics were even harder on the contactees. Scientists, air force investigators, and others pointed out numerous seemingly weak, unconvincing, or even absurd elements in contactee stories. For example, nearly all the alien beings depicted in these accounts appeared to be ordinary humans, and members of the Caucasian race to boot, who could breathe earthly air and speak perfect English. According to biologists, the evolution of life on other planets, as on earth, would be driven by trillions of random circumstances and events taking place over the course of hundreds of millions of years. Even under earthlike planetary conditions, these numerous variables would not likely repeat themselves in any specific order. So the chances of extraterrestrial beings evolving into forms very similar to those of contemporary humans are slim to nonexistent.

Skeptics also took issue with the contactees' descriptions of various planets and moons, especially after the advent of human space flight in the 1960s and 1970s. George Adamski's claim that the far side of earth's moon supported an atmosphere, lakes of water, and cities was proved to be false when Soviet and U.S. spacecraft flew around the moon. Photographs of the far side revealed a lifeless, cratered surface essentially no different from the one facing earth. Also, using satellite probes, in the 1970s and 1980s scientists showed that Venus, Mars, and Jupiter, frequently cited as the home worlds of the "space brothers," were all inhospitable to life of any known variety.

In addition, skeptics argued that what little evidence the contactees used to support their claims was bogus. For example, Adamski had published photos of the saucer he supposedly had ridden in.

A photo of the far side of the moon reveals an airless, barren landscape. George Adamski had earlier claimed that the far side had an atmosphere, as well as forests, lakes, and cities.

After close examination, investigators showed that the saucer depicted was actually a model constructed of parts from human-made chicken brooding devices and bottle coolers. When skeptics rejected Daniel Fry's contact stories, he offered to take a lie detector test. He failed the test and then, in an indignant huff, claimed that someone had rigged the machine against him. Some contactees were even jailed. After convincing thousands of people to give them money to construct their own flying saucer, a Nebraska contactee named Rheinholdt Schmidt and a colleague received prison sentences.

If the contactees were fakers, some of their devotees asked, what possible motivation did they have for misleading people? Skeptics answered that personal notoriety and money were probable motivations. In addition, some contactee stories might have been sincere attempts to create peace and harmony in a world filled with war and anxiety. The space brothers invariably came from planets where strife, poverty, and unhappiness had been eradicated, places the contactees hoped would serve as models for a "new earth." It was this message of peace and harmony, delivered with religious overtones, writes skeptic Curtis Peebles, which held the central role in the contactee myth. "They" had selected the contactee to carry out this "Christ-like" mission to earth. The contactees never said they were the son of God with God's word. They did claim to have been selected by angelic, superior beings from heavenlike planets. The contactee myth can be thought of as a messiah-based religion for an age when traditional religion has lost its meaning.

A number of skeptics have also been quick to point out the similarities in the major contactee stories to the characters and plot of a popular 1951 Hollywood film: *The Day the Earth Stood Still*, starring Michael Rennie and Patricia Neal and directed by Robert Wise. Rennie played Klaatu, a tall, dignified-looking, and very human alien who came to earth with a warning for humanity. The advanced races on nearby planets, he said, would not tolerate the spread of nuclear bombs and other destructive human technology into outer space. Klaatu befriended an American woman, played by Neal, who, like the contactees, felt compelled to help save her own kind. Hostile soldiers shot and killed Klaatu. Yet, with the aid of superior technology, he rose, Christlike, from the dead, delivered his warning, and was transported into the sky. (Further strengthening the messianic parallel was the name Klaatu used when hiding in human society—"Mr. Carpenter" was an obvious reference to the craft in which Jesus of Nazareth was trained, as stated in the Bible.) "Because the themes in the film were so much like later contactee literature," David Jacobs remarks, "it is possible that some contactees may have drawn upon the film as a source for their ideas."

Old Versus New Contactees

Despite frequent debunking by both skeptics and believers, new contactees have appeared almost every year. And some of the classic contactees still maintain considerable followings, even long after

> "I felt like a child in the presence of one with great wisdom and much love, and I became very humble within myself . . . for from him was radiating a feeling of infinite understanding and kindness, with supreme humility."
>
> George Adamski, *Inside the Space Ships*

> "[The contactee] regards himself definitely as having been 'chosen' and utterly disregards . . . the statistical improbability that one person, on a random basis, should be able to have many repeated UFO experiences . . . while the majority of humanity lives out a lifetime without having even one UFO experience."
>
> J. Allen Hynek, *The UFO Experience: A Scientific Inquiry*

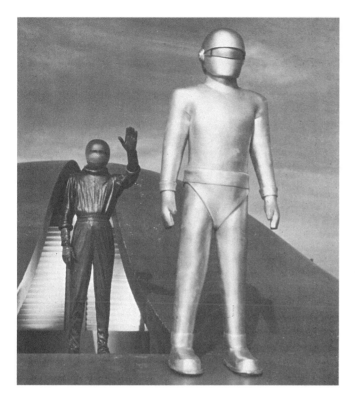

In this scene from the 1951 film *The Day the Earth Stood Still*, space brother Klaatu (rear) raises his hand in a gesture of greeting to humanity, while the robot policeman Gort (forerunner of Robocop?) menacingly stands guard.

their deaths. The George Adamski Foundation, for instance, is alive and well in California in the 1990s and has thousands of members worldwide. In England, a group called the Star Fellowship keeps Adamski's memory alive and advocates his beliefs about humanity belonging to a brotherhood of alien races.

However, in recent years the old-style contactees and their followers have had to compete for attention with the publicity surrounding a newer kind of contactee. One major element of the old contactee stories was the free will of the contactees themselves. The aliens always extended cordial invitations to enter and ride their saucers. By contrast, the "abductees," constituting a widespread and compelling element of the saucer phenomenon, claim to have been taken aboard such craft against their will.

Four

Interrupted Journeys: The Saucer Abduction Phenomenon

The contactee phenomenon had attracted a solid following of tens of thousands of people. But contactee reports, literature, and debates were eventually overshadowed by the flying saucer abduction phenomenon, which captured the imaginations of tens of millions. The "abduction era," which has continued to the present, began on September 19, 1961. On that evening, Betty and Barney Hill, a Portsmouth, New Hampshire, couple, were driving on a desolate mountain road on their way home from a trip to Canada. Suddenly, they saw a "light" in the sky that they felt was following them. According to the Hills' later account, the couple soon found themselves surrounded by small humanoid creatures with large eyes and slitlike mouths. The beings took the people into a disklike saucer and there performed "experiments" on them, including probes of Barney's genitals and Betty's navel. The beings showed Betty a screen with a "star map" on it and finally released her and her husband.

When the Hills reported their strange experience, the initial reactions were lukewarm. Not surprisingly, since direct contact with aliens had been claimed, most people who reviewed the case automatically lumped it with the contactee reports.

(Opposite page) Betty and Barney Hill, whose alleged 1961 experience with a flying saucer and its occupants launched the "abduction era."

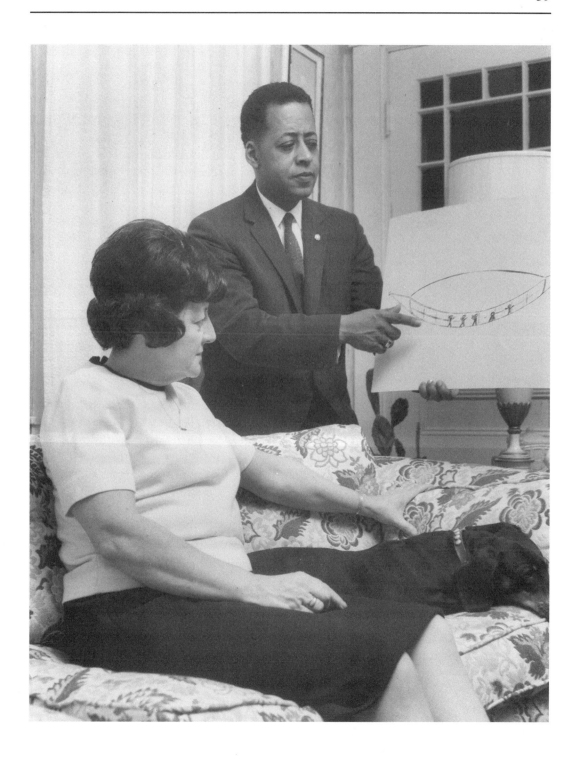

Popular writer Frank Edwards, for example, included the Hills' story in the chapter on Adamski and other contactees in his 1968 book, *Flying Saucers—Here and Now!* Conservative believers such as Donald Keyhoe and most others at NICAP, by then fed up with contactee stories, flatly refused to accept the Hills' claims to have been abducted.

However, a few people were very intrigued with the Hills' story. One of them was John G. Fuller, a columnist for *Saturday Review* magazine, who wrote an entire book about the case. Titled *The Interrupted Journey*, the book appeared in 1966 and widely publicized the Hills and their reported close encounter of the third kind. The case proved to be a harbinger of things to come. Abduction cases soon became the most frequently reported in the saucer literature, far exceeding and, indeed, almost replacing traditional reports involving encounters of the first and second kinds.

Two Missing Hours

What made the Hills' case the classic abduction story was that the basic elements of their story set a pattern that was to be repeated in a majority of later abduction cases. Among these often-reported elements were the small beings with large eyes inhabiting saucerlike craft, the kidnapping of humans, and the performing of medical experiments on the victims. Two other classic and crucial elements of the Hills' experience were the process of hypnosis and the concept of "missing time." According to the Hills, when they arrived home on the night of September 19, 1961, they remembered only that they had seen a strange craft with windows through which "occupants" stared out at them. Then, Betty began having nightmares. She envisioned herself and her husband being kidnapped, forced into the saucer, and probed by the occupants. Barney tried to reconstruct their experience and discovered that the journey from Canada had taken two hours longer

"I feel I was abducted. . . . I don't want to believe I was abducted, so I say I feel because this makes it comfortable for me to accept something I don't want to accept that happened."

Abductee Barney Hill under hypnosis, as reported by J. Allen Hynek, in *The UFO Experience: A Scientific Inquiry*

"[The UFOs'] existence as concrete objects is of less concern to me than the experiences of these two people showing the cumulative impact of past experiences and fantasies on their present experiences and responses."

Boston psychiatrist Dr. Benjamin Simon on his patients, professed abductees Betty and Barney Hill

The sketch Barney Hill later made of one of the strange little beings he claimed abducted him and his wife.

than it should have. What had happened during those "missing" hours, they wondered?

The Hills went to a Boston psychiatrist, Dr. Benjamin Simon, who employed the process of "hypnotic regression," or the use of hypnosis to discover information buried deep in the subconscious mind. Under hypnosis, the Hills described their abduction in great detail. The account revealed how the beings had done something to make Betty and Barney "forget" the experience. Dr. Simon's conclusion was that the Hills had seen something that had disturbed them, possibly the unknown flying object that they had consciously remembered. Their fears, combined with what they had read and heard in the media about flying saucers and alien beings, then stimulated a fantasy experience in Betty's dreams. But Fuller and other investigators did not buy this explanation. They held that the Hills were stable,

Another of Barney Hill's sketches, this one depicting the alien craft he said he encountered.

reliable witnesses who had seen and experienced something real, not imaginary.

Real or not, the Hills' case turned out to be very similar in many respects to others. One such case had occurred much earlier, in 1957, but was not publicized or studied until the mid-1960s. It involved a Brazilian farmer named Antonio Villas Boas. According to Boas, five small aliens chased and captured him, forced him into their "egg-shaped" craft, and took a blood sample from his chin. A small alien woman then had sexual intercourse with him and afterward indicated that he had made her pregnant.

The Andreasson Case

Another famous abduction case occurred in 1967, only months after the publication of *The Interrupted Journey*. A Massachusetts woman named Betty Andreasson claimed that on January 25 four small creatures with large heads, no noses, slitlike mouths, and large almond-shaped eyes had abducted her. She had been taken into their oval-shaped craft and had painful medical experiments performed on her. Richard Williams summarizes Andreasson's recollections:

> A probe was pushed up her nose. She reported: "I heard something break, like a membrane or a vein or something, like a piece of tissue they broke through." Another probe was inserted in her navel. . . . Next she was made to sit in a glass

chair, where she was enclosed by a transparent cover and immersed in fluid; she could breathe through tubes attached to her mouth and nose. A sweet liquid oozed into her mouth. When she was released from the chair, she found that she had traveled to the aliens' planet. Two of the creatures took her along a tunnel and through a series of chambers. The first was full of small reptile-like creatures; the second was a large green-colored space, where they floated over pyramids to a city of mysterious crystalline forms.

As in the Hill case, the aliens caused Andreasson to forget her experience. Only after undergoing hypnosis ten years later, she claims, did she remember all the disturbing details.

During Andreasson's ten-year period of memory loss, the number of annually reported cases of abduction began to increase. In October 1975 NBC

Well-known abductee Betty Andreasson undergoes hypnosis, part of a process of remembering her abduction ordeal, as UFO investigator Joseph Santangelo listens.

Television broadcast a movie dramatization of the Hill case titled *The UFO Incident*, a program that attracted a large viewing audience. Two weeks after this broadcast, an Arizona forestry worker named Travis Walton disappeared after attempting to investigate a strange flying object he and his coworkers had sighted. After six days, Walton reappeared and claimed he had been abducted by aliens. In November 1979 a young Frenchman named Franck Fontaine disappeared near Paris after two friends reported that a "huge ball of light" had engulfed his car. When Fontaine resurfaced seven days later, he said he could not remember what had happened to him. But over the course of many weeks he recalled being kidnapped and taken inside a flying saucer.

An artist's conception depicts Travis Walton attempting to defend himself against the aliens who he claimed abducted him.

These stories were not unique. By 1976, fifty such abduction cases had been reported and only four years later that number had risen to more than two hundred.

A Repeated and Recognizable Pattern

Because of the large and growing number of abduction cases, some researchers became convinced that at least a sizable portion of the abductees were a part of a very real phenomenon. A number of investigators pointed out that the many common traits these stories shared formed a recognizable pattern. For instance, in his thoughtful study of abduction cases, *Abductions: Human Encounters with Aliens*, Pulitzer Prize–winning author John E. Mack wrote that in the typical case

> the abductee is commonly "floated" . . . down the hall, through the wall or windows of the house, or through the roof of the car. . . . Usually the experiencer [abductee] is accompanied by one, two, or more humanoid beings who guide them to the [space] ship. At some point early in this process the experiencer discovers that he or she has been numbed or totally paralyzed by a touch of the hand or an instrument held by one of the beings. . . . The UFOs vary in size from a few feet across to several hundred yards wide. They are described as silvery or metallic and cigar-, saucer-, or dome-shaped. . . . Often the abductee will struggle. . . . to stop the experience, but this does little good except to give the individual a vital sense that he or she is not simply a passive victim.

In addition to these frequently reported and shared elements in abduction stories, a new twist in the abduction phenomenon appeared in the late 1970s and early 1980s. Some people who did not claim to have seen a flying saucer or alien being sought psychiatric help because they said they were afraid of certain objects, or places, such as a deserted stretch of road. But once hypnotized, they

"The Travis Walton case is one of the most important and intriguing in the history of the UFO phenomena."

Spokesperson for Aerial Phenomena Research Organization (APRO)

"Based on [Travis Walton's] reactions on all [polygraph] charts, it is the opinion of this examiner that Walton, in concert with others, is attempting to perpetrate a UFO hoax, and that he has not been on any spacecraft."

Official government-employed Arizona polygraph examiner John J. McCarthy

Flying saucer investigator and "believer" Budd Hopkins, who published his study of UFO abductees, *Missing Time*, in 1981.

described being abducted by aliens. This suggested that a person, indeed any person, might have been an abductee and have no conscious memory of the ordeal.

This new twist led some investigators to propose a startling theory. Perhaps saucer abductions were not isolated cases, but rather, involved tens of thousands of unknowing people. Budd Hopkins, a New York artist turned saucer investigator and believer, interviewed and studied many abductees and published his conclusions in his 1981 book, *Missing Time*. Hopkins suggested that "a very long-term, in-depth study is being made [by aliens] of a relatively large sample of humans." In Hopkins scenario, the victims are first abducted as young children and implanted with monitoring devices. The aliens soon release the abductees and keep remote track of them until they reach sexual maturity. Then they abduct the victims again and reexamine them.

Hopkins continued studying abduction cases throughout the1980s and became convinced that the beings the abductees described were very real. He emphasized this point in his second book, *Intruders*, published in 1987, writing, "None of these recollections [of alien abductors] in any way suggests traditional sci-fi gods and devils . . . the aliens are described neither as all-powerful, lordly presences, nor as satanic monsters, but instead as complex, controlling, physically frail beings." These beings became known as the "grays," in reference to the frequent descriptions of their gray skin.

Thousands of Abductees?

Writer Whitley Strieber said he became involved in studying abduction cases after he himself was abducted from his house in New York State. He described his experiences in his best-selling 1987 book, *Communion*. Strieber agrees with Hopkins that many thousands of people of all walks of life have been victims of abduction and do not even know it. Commenting on the hundreds of letters he received from readers, Strieber said:

> Most of the letters are as striking for their articulate style as for their astonishing content. Eighty-eight percent of the letters describe some sort of "visitor" experience. About 40 percent report an actual abduction.

Regarding the aliens' motivation for abducting so many people, believers have varied opinions. Most theories involve genetic or reproductive experiments of some kind, perhaps to create a new and better race of humans, or to help revitalize a dying alien race. Hopkins suggests that the aliens are conducting genetic experiments as part of an effort to produce alien/human hybrids.

Frauds and Imaginary Narratives

Despite the large number of saucer abduction cases and the convincing tone of some of them, many skeptics believe that the phenomenon is not real. First, they say, many abduction reports are hoaxes, staged for publicity or other reasons. For example, one of the most celebrated of these reports, that of Travis Walton, did not hold up well under close examination. Four days after Walton returned from his alleged close encounter, he took a "lie detector" test administered by Arizona's leading polygraph examiner, who called the young man's responses a "gross deception" and the most obvious example of lying he had seen in twenty years. Philip Klass investigated the case. He got Walton to admit to having watched *The UFO Incident* on TV only two weeks before his abduction. Klass believes the program inspired Walton and his friends to stage their own UFO incident. Similarly, the renowned French abduction case involving Franck Fontaine fell apart when one of Fontaine's friends admitted that "We staged the whole thing to get a little money."

Still, most skeptics agree that a large number of abduction cases are not out-and-out frauds because the "victims" really do believe the events they describe took place. This certainly seemed to be true in cases like those of the Hills and Betty Andreasson. However, say skeptical investigators, such events could well have been inadvertently manufactured in the abductees' minds. In this view, unhappy, troubled, or disturbed persons might unknowingly work out their anxieties by transferring the blame for their problems to others—in this case saucers and aliens. The peculiar and consistent images and details of the spaceships and beings are already present in a potential abductee's mind. This, say Klass, Peebles,

Flying saucer skeptics suspect that Travis Walton (pictured) faked his widely publicized abduction, possibly after watching a TV movie based on the Hill case.

1761-41

and others, is the result of a constant barrage of such images in sci-fi books and magazines; TV programs such as *Star Trek*, *The Outer Limits*, *The Invaders*, and *The Twilight Zone;* and movies, including *Invaders from Mars*, in which sinister aliens kidnap humans and implant devices in their heads, *This Island Earth* and *Earth vs. the Flying Saucers*, both of which feature the abduction theme, and a large number of films dealing with cross-breeding between humans and aliens.

Also, skeptics point out, hypnosis, a key tool in piecing together abduction stories, may not be as objective and reliable as many people suppose. In

In this scene from the movie *This Island Earth*, humans who have been kidnapped by aliens from the planet Metaluna are menaced by an insectlike Metalunan "mutant."

1977 Dr. Alvin H. Lawson, of California State University at Long Beach, conducted a revealing study. Lawson and his colleagues asked a group of people who said they knew little about the topic of flying saucers and aliens to undergo hypnosis. Once hypnotized, the subjects were asked to imagine themselves being abducted by extraterrestrials. Lawson and the others were surprised when they compared the resulting stories with those from people who really claimed to have been abducted and got nearly an exact match. "It is clear from the imaginary narratives," commented Lawson,

> that a great many apparent patterns may originate in the mind and so be available to a witness—whether imaginary or "real." If a person who is totally uninformed about UFOs suddenly [is asked to pretend to be the victim of an abduction], it seems safe to assume that the individual's own sensibility will be able to provide under hypnotic regression, pattern details of his encounter which he may or may not have actually experienced in a "real" sense.

The results of Lawson's tests, remarks Peebles, show "not that there was a massive number of covert abductions. Rather, it shows that nearly anyone can, under hypnosis, provide an abduction story." This might explain why cases of alleged abduction now number in the tens of thousands. Most abductees and abduction believers have either ignored or rejected the results of Lawson's study.

From Kind and Humane to Sinister and Controlling

Another objection to the abduction phenomenon voiced by some skeptics is that, like earlier flying saucer phenomena, it seems closely to mirror changing social attitudes. For example, Peebles points out, in the contactee era of the 1950s most people had a positive attitude toward authority figures. In those days science seemed to offer human-

"The contactees had their own 'relationship,' rooted in the world view of the 1950s. When this faded, it was replaced, in the 1960s and 1970s, by the abduction myth, yet another attempt to find a relationship with mythological beings."

Writer and saucer skeptic Curtis Peebles, *Watch the Skies!: A Chronicle of the Flying Saucer Myth*

"Somewhere, somehow [aided by experiments on abductees], human beings—or possibly hybrids of some sort—are being produced by a technology . . . superior to ours."

Abduction proponent Budd Hopkins, *Intruders: The Incredible Visitations at Copley Woods*

ity hope for a more progressive, happier future, and President Dwight Eisenhower projected a kind, grandfatherly image. Not surprisingly, the aliens depicted by the contactees were kind, humane, and concerned that technology be used in beneficial ways. By contrast, since the late 1970s authority figures have increasingly come to be seen as corrupt, controlling, and abusive. And in many people's minds science seems more dangerous, invasive, and antihuman. Correspondingly, the aliens depicted in abduction stories are cold, sinister, controlling, and inhumane.

Believers typically counter the skeptics by asserting that the early contactees were mainly fakes and disturbed people and so should not be lumped together with the abductees. According to some believers, changing social attitudes did not propagate abduction cases. It is entirely possible, they say, that such cases began to be reported in the 1960s and 1970s because that is when the aliens chose to begin large-scale experiments on humans. The increasing distrust for authority may be in part a result of the way government officials have handled saucer and abduction cases. In fact, say a majority of believers, the government knows much more about these cases than it admits and is involved in a massive cover-up. And that charge, true or not, is a story unto itself.

Five

The Conspiracy Theory: Is the Government Hiding the Truth?

(Opposite page) This picture supposedly shows a flying saucer sighted over Passaic, New Jersey, in 1952. At the time, the idea of a government conspiracy to cover up the truth about such craft was already taking hold in the popular consciousness.

Almost from the beginning of the modern flying saucer era, some believers were convinced that the U.S. government knew more about the phenomenon than it claimed to know. The air force, through its projects Sign, Grudge, and Blue Book, was the agency that conducted the saucer investigations. Consequently, it was the initial target of frequent charges of withholding information about flying saucers. Air force officials steadfastly maintained that these charges were unfounded. Typical was a statement made by an air force spokesperson in 1952: "One thing I would like to do is dispel the belief of some that we are holding something back. We are not."

But a growing number of citizens, spearheaded by leaders and members of believer groups such as NICAP, regarded such disclaimers with suspicion. As David Jacobs explains, no matter what assurances the air force gave about its motives and actions,

it could not convince UFO proponents to accept at face value statements about its objectivity and openness. The Air Force refused to declassify [release from secrecy] its sighting reports and thus found itself in a dilemma. . . . By refuting the secrecy charges while at the same time refusing to declassify the sighting reports, the

Air Force incurred even greater criticism and appeared to be covering up as the critics charged.

As to why the air force might be holding back, believers offered varied opinions. One of the most widely held was articulated by self-described contactee Orfeo Angelucci, who wrote that releasing the "truth" about the saucers "would be the beginning of national panic that no amount of sane reasoning could quell."

As time went on, the charges of an air force cover-up became increasingly loud and angry. As perceived by believers, this cover-up grew more sinister and disturbing, and also became larger in scope, spreading beyond the air force brass to many other military and government agencies. With each passing decade, the alleged government conspiracy about flying saucers appeared more widespread, more frightening, and more dangerous.

Unwarranted Secrecy?

The saucer conspiracy theory began in earnest in the early 1950s. At the time, the investigative agency that eventually became Project Blue Book had a staff of only five or six people, two of whom were secretaries. As a result, the agency found it physically impossible to investigate every saucer report, which meant that many reports received little or no attention. In addition, the agency kept most of its findings classified. It did this, it stated, to protect both witnesses' identities and the nature of certain new electronic devices it used in its investigations. It was these practices—the failure to study all "unknown" cases and the refusal to declassify documents—that initially made some believers doubt the validity of the air force saucer studies.

Believers also became suspicious when the air force repeatedly asserted that it could find no evidence that the saucers were mysterious, hostile, or even piloted. In 1952, for instance, shortly after he

This photo, taken in the 1960s, shows the staff of Project Blue Book, including its director, Hector Quintanilla (seated).

took charge of Project Blue Book, Edward Ruppelt announced the results of his first set of findings:

> Out of about 4,000 people who said they saw a "flying saucer," sufficiently detailed descriptions were given in only 12 cases. Having culled [singled out and examined] the cream of the crop, it was impossible to develop a picture of what a "flying saucer" is. . . . Therefore . . . it is considered to be highly improbable that any of the reports of unidentified aerial objects examined in this study represent observations of technological development outside the range of present-day scientific knowledge.

Later, in 1955, the air force released what it called "Special Report Number 14," which summarized a statistical study conducted by a private institute at the government's request. The report stated, "On the basis of this study it is believed that all the unidentified aerial objects could have been explained if more complete observational data had been available." And in 1957 the air force released a more sweeping statement. Based on ten years of investigations,

Well-known flying saucer
"believer" Donald Keyhoe
holds a copy of his 1953
book, *Flying Saucers from
Outer Space*, just one of
several works he wrote on
the subject in the 1950s and
1960s.

officials said, no evidence existed that the saucer "unknowns" were "hostile," "interplanetary space-ships," or "a threat to the security of the country."

But a number of believers were not satisfied with these official statements. The most prominent early proponent of the theory of an air force cover-up was Donald Keyhoe. Typical of his repeated charges was, "The Air Force has withheld and is still withholding information on UFOs. NICAP intends to secure all possible verified factual evidence and . . . to end unwarranted secrecy." Keyhoe's 1953 book, *Flying Saucers from Outer Space*, sold more than 500,000 copies, a huge number at the time, and brought the supposed cover-up to the public's attention.

Not long afterward, Keyhoe expanded the scope of his cover-up charge by claiming that other government agencies were also involved. In a letter to the director of another believer group, he stated, "Actually, the Air Force is not the only agency involved; the CIA, National Security Council, FBI, Civil Defense, all are tied in at top levels. The White House, of course, will have the final word as to what people are to be told, and when." Keyhoe developed this theme still further in his third book, *The Flying Saucer Conspiracy,* published in 1955. He described a shadowy government "silence group" that was in charge of the conspiracy.

The Condon Report

The air force publicly and flatly denied the charges of a cover-up. In private statements, other agencies implicated by Keyhoe did the same. Skeptics who have examined the charges over the years, including Menzel, Klass, and Peebles, have pointed out that Keyhoe offered no tangible evidence for his conspiracy theory. Indeed, stated Peebles, the descriptions of the government "silence group" were "a figment of Keyhoe's own imagination." The skeptics suggested that Keyhoe and his supporters had approached the subject with a built-in bias. Instead of studying the evidence and then forming a conclusion, they had begun by accepting as fact the notion that the saucers were from other worlds. Thus, they would naturally distrust any findings refuting their central principle.

Countering this argument, Keyhoe and other conspiracy advocates held that ample evidence existed for distrusting both the government *and* well-known skeptics like Menzel. The skeptics, said Keyhoe, were either well-meaning but naïve individuals who did not know what was really going on, or part of the conspiracy. As for the government, Keyhoe charged, air force officials had blatantly shown their own bias. They had frequently ignored,

"The evidence presented on Unidentified Flying Objects shows no indication that these phenomena constitute a direct physical threat to [U.S.] national security. We firmly believe that . . . there is no evidence that the phenomena indicate a need for the revision of current scientific concepts."

Official air force statement, January 17, 1953

"Behind a new curtain of secrecy, the U.S. Air Force is engaged in a dangerous gamble involving attacks on UFOs. Despite AF denials, unidentified flying objects are still operating in our skies."

Donald E. Keyhoe, *Aliens from Space: The Real Story of Unidentified Flying Objects*

discounted, or discredited the testimony of reliable witnesses who were certain that the "saucers" they had seen were piloted craft. In one of his later books, Keyhoe declared:

> The time has come to stop the long deception, the deliberate discrediting of thousands of honest witnesses. At any time, there could be a sudden development for which we [the public] are totally unprepared. The secrecy, the censorship must be stopped. We must end the dangerous gamble which could involve us all.

Throughout the 1950s and on into the 1960s, Keyhoe and other prominent believers, aided by many concerned citizens, continued demanding that the air force "tell the truth" about flying saucers. The controversy came to a head between 1966 and 1969. Public demand for answers about the saucers became so great that Congress conducted a brief hearing on the matter. This, in turn, forced the air

"STAY CALM, DR. CONDON—JUST TELL THEM YOU DON'T BELIEVE IN THEM!"

force to commission a group of unbiased civilian scientists to study the saucer phenomenon. Heading the group was Dr. Edward U. Condon, an internationally known physicist. On January 9, 1969, after nearly three years of study, Condon's committee released its findings, which became known as the Condon Report. The report stated:

> Our general conclusion is that nothing has come from the study of UFOs in the past 21 years that has added to scientific knowledge. Careful consideration of the record as it is available to us leads us to conclude that further extensive study of UFOs probably cannot be justified in the expectation that science will be advanced thereby.

Reactions to the Condon Report were mixed. Many scientists, newspapers, and magazines praised the study. Typical was a review in the journal *Science*, which called it the "most thorough and sophisticated investigation of the nebulous [mysterious] UFO phenomenon ever conducted." On the opposite side, Keyhoe, as expected, rejected the committee's findings. Although he had at first thrown NICAP's support behind the study group, he later withdrew that support and called the final report "biased and superficial." But Keyhoe was not alone. Physicist James McDonald, who had blasted Project Blue Book, criticized the report for analyzing only a few and, in his opinion, the least mysterious of the saucer sightings. J. Allen Hynek agreed, charging that the committee had "grossly underestimated the scope and nature" of the flying saucer phenomenon.

Project Blue Book Shuts Down

The controversy intensified further when the Condon Report's findings led to the ax falling on Project Blue Book. On December 17, 1969, the secretary of the air force announced the agency's closing, stating, "The continuation of Project Blue

Dr. Edward Condon, who headed a committee of civilian scientists organized in the late 1960s to study the UFO phenomenon.

Book cannot be justified either on the ground of national security or in the interest of science." According to the government, Blue Book was shutting down to save taxpayer money from being wasted on frivolous investigations. But Keyhoe and many others vehemently disagreed, charging that the agency's closing was part of the conspiracy. The air force, they said, planned to continue with its secret investigations of the saucers and to hide what it already knew to be true—that they were piloted alien craft.

Rumors of Crashed Saucers

The conspiracy theory continued to gain momentum in the 1970s and on into the early 1980s as the abductee era gathered steam. Many believers came to feel that the large number of abduction cases, coupled with the government's silence on the subject, strongly hinted at a cover-up. With so many people being abducted, they asked, how could the government have failed to detect and intercept some of the saucers and their occupants? The answer, according to this view, was that it had *not* failed to do so. Rumors began to surface about secret government projects devoted to the examination of crashed or captured saucers.

In 1974, for example, a NICAP spokesperson charged that the air force was keeping two saucers and twelve alien bodies in deep freeze at Wright-Patterson Air Force Base in Dayton, Ohio. Base officials said they wanted to dispel what they called a "wild rumor." So they allowed members of the public to tour the infamous "Hangar 18," the building in which the extraterrestrial relics were supposedly stored. When the inspection revealed nothing incriminating, believers charged that the air force had merely moved the evidence somewhere else.

While believers lacked the hard evidence to support their charges about Hangar 18, they felt they had such evidence in another similar case. In 1980,

**Naturally, there was a bit of skepticism
among the media regarding the
official Air Force explanation.**

writers Charles Berlitz and William L. Moore published *The Roswell Incident*, which centered on a little-known saucer case from the early postwar years, when today's U.S. Air Force was still known as the Army Air Force, or AAF. In July 1947, AAF officials announced that they had discovered debris from a crashed "flying disk" near Roswell, New Mexico. The next day, they said that they had been mistaken. Thereafter the official explanation was that the debris had come from a downed weather balloon.

Berlitz and Moore claimed that the balloon story was part of a cover-up and that the AAF had actually recovered sections of an alien saucer and the corpses of four of its small occupants. Among the proofs they cited was the later testimony of Major Jesse A. Marcel, the principal investigator on the case. Shortly before his death in 1978, Marcel claimed that the debris he had examined was "nothing made on earth." He said that a tinfoil-like substance in the debris remained unaffected after assaults by blowtorches and sledgehammers.

In an attempt to rebut these claims, some skeptics say that Berlitz and Moore's historical context for the case is faulty. According to Curtis Peebles:

> The events took place only two weeks after Arnold saw the nine disks. In early July 1947, no one—not the Army Air Force, not the FBI, not the public, not the believers—had any idea what the "flying disks" were. The two leading theories were U.S. and Soviet secret weapons. The extraterrestrial hypothesis did not become popular until the following year. . . . When Roswell AAF issued the press release, there was no reason to connect the debris with alien spaceships. Decades later, when Roswell was rediscovered [by Berlitz and Moore], it had to conform to all the elements of the flying saucer myth—disk-shaped alien spaceships, little aliens, and, of course, the government cover-up—all of which sprang up *after* 1947.

Many believers have remained undeterred by such attempts to explain away the Roswell incident. The case has continued to be one of the strongest and most popular arguments for a government conspiracy to suppress information about flying saucers.

Damning Accusations

In the wake of the initial controversy surrounding Berlitz and Moore's book about Roswell, both the government and the saucer skeptics found themselves increasingly under attack. Accusations against the government became more numerous and more damning, as believers described a conspiracy of massive and sinister proportions. Later in 1980, for instance, a source who would identify himself only as "Mike" claimed that the air force was conducting flight tests of a flying saucer at "Area 51," a secret base near Groom Lake, Nevada. The air force denied any such tests and insisted that it possessed no crashed saucers.

Another development in the conspiracy controversy occurred in 1987. On May 29 of that year a Los Angeles TV producer released two documents, thereafter referred to as the "MJ-12 documents," given to her by "an unidentified source." The papers allegedly dated from 1947 and 1952. The first appeared to be a memo signed by President Harry Truman authorizing the secretary of defense to set up a secret agency called "Majestic 12" to study the downed Roswell saucer and other such cases. The second paper purported to be a top-secret briefing about the MJ-12 group for the new president-elect Dwight Eisenhower.

The MJ-12 documents remain a topic of heated debate. In 1990, after an exhaustive study, Philip Klass announced his contention that the papers were forgeries. He claimed that they had been typed on a typewriter manufactured in 1963, many years after their supposed issue. Believers split into two camps. Some maintain that Klass was wrong and that the papers are authentic. Others agree that there was a hoax but pin it on the CIA, saying that the government had another, supersecret group investigating flying saucers, and the intelligence agency had perpetrated the MJ-12 scam in a deliberate attempt to divert attention from the government's "real" research.

Not long after the appearance of the MJ-12 documents came the first of the "whistle-blowers." These are people, some of them former government

"We have, indeed, been contacted . . . by extraterrestrial beings, and the U.S. government, in collusion with the other national powers of the earth, is determined to keep this information from the general public. The purpose of the international conspiracy is to maintain a workable stability among the nations of the world and for them, in turn, to retain institutional control over their respective populations."

Former CIA official Victor Marchetti, in *Second Look* magazine, May 1979

"The alien myth is nihilistic [negative and destructive], and rests not on independent inquiry, but on the revealed truth of the whistle-blower. It is not considered polite to point out the contradictions in the stories. One does not ask who takes out the garbage at Dulce [N.M.]."

Curtis Peebles, *Watch the Skies!: A Chronicle of the Flying Saucer Myth*

John Lear, one of the so-called whistle-blowers, who insists that a massive government conspiracy designed to keep knowledge about alien visitations from the public is under way.

employees, who say that they feel it their duty to expose the government's "secret saucer conspiracy." One whistle-blower, John Lear, claimed that the U.S. government had "sold out" the human race to the aliens. In a despicable deal with these beings, he said, the government agreed to ignore or cover up many abduction cases in exchange for alien technology. According to Lear, the aliens are partly motivated by their need for "hormonal secretions" from humans and other earth animals to correct a genetic digestive disorder.

In 1989 Lear and another whistle-blower, Milton William Cooper, issued a formal "Indictment" of the U.S. government. They demanded that the president and other top officials

> cease aiding and abetting and concealing this Alien Nation which exists within our borders. We charge the government to cease all operations, projects, treaties, and any other involvement with this Alien Nation. We charge the government to order this Alien Nation and all of its members to leave the United States and this Earth immediately, now and for all time.

Cooper went on to make a long list of extraordinary claims, including the notions that the "grays" had created the human race and had been manipulating it for thousands of years; that the Americans and the Soviets, while helping the aliens, had long been trying to develop weapons to stop them; and that when President John F. Kennedy had threatened to reveal everything, the MJ-12 group had had him assassinated. According to Cooper, seed money for this research had been raised by the U.S. government, which, aided by oil company executives including future president George Bush, had cornered the world's illegal drug market.

A Huge Question Mark

Government officials have steadfastly denied all such charges. And skeptics ranging from Klass and

Peebles to the respected French astronomer Jacques Vallée have called such ideas "ridiculous" and "wild ravings." Yet Cooper and several other whistle-blowers developed and maintain a devoted following. Their vision of a massive conspiracy involving alien races and world governments has recently achieved a new burst of popularity in the success of the television show *The X Files*. The program traces the adventures of two FBI agents who continuously uncover evidence of the grand conspiracy, only to have other government agents destroy or conceal that evidence.

Not all saucer believers accept the idea of a conspiracy as far-reaching and evil as the one the whistle-blowers propose. Yet many people around the world suspect that their governments know more about flying saucers than they admit. In the late 1980s, for example, 50 percent of Americans interviewed in a Gallup poll said they believed that flying saucers were from other worlds. A large proportion apparently believe that some sort of government cover-up is possible or likely. The U.S. government, like other governments, continues to assert that no cover-up or conspiracy exists. For the moment, a huge question mark hangs over the issue, and the debate goes on. Both believers and skeptics look to the future expectantly, each hoping that absolute and unarguable proof will emerge at last to validate their respective positions.

"We further charge the government to make a complete disclosure of its alien involvement to the American people . . . and to make a full accounting for its actions."

Whistle-blowers Milton William Cooper and John Lear in their 1989 "Indictment" of the U.S. government

"Who takes out the garbage?"

French astronomer Jacques Vallée responding to the whistle-blowers' claims that an underground alien base the size of Manhattan exists in Dulce, New Mexico

Six

From the Mundane to the Bizarre: Explanations for Flying Saucers

The literature of the modern flying saucer era consists of quite literally tens of thousands of reports of close encounters of the first, second, and third kinds. These have ranged from sightings of strange objects and lights in the sky to alleged abductions that involved experimentation on the victims. The saucer literature is also filled with books, articles, and studies attempting to sift through, categorize, analyze, and explain the many reported saucer incidents.

The central question in this vast collection of reports and speculative writings about them has always been straightforward. Are the saucers piloted craft from beyond earth or do reports of them constitute misinterpretations of more mundane earthly phenomena? Skeptics often go to great lengths to explain how natural phenomena—ball lightning, for instance—can, under the right conditions, easily be mistaken for flying craft. Most skeptics are especially doubtful about reports of contact with flesh-and-blood aliens. As famous skeptic Isaac Asimov put it:

> Any extraterrestrials reported are always described as essentially human in form, which is so unlikely a possibility that we can dismiss it out of hand. Descriptions of the ship itself and of

(Opposite page) Wave clouds float over South Georgia, one of the Falkland Islands off the east coast of South America. Odd natural phenomena such as this may be the explanation for at least some flying saucer sightings.

the scientific devices of the aliens usually betray a great knowledge of science fiction movies of the more primitive kind and no knowledge whatever of real science.

Cutting through all the analysis and explanation, however, skeptics usually fall back on their bottom-line argument: not a single piece of hard evidence has ever been presented to authenticate an extraterrestrial origin for the saucers. Hard evidence would consist of a piece of metal, cloth, or some other material that scientists could test in a lab and show conclusively to be of a nonearthly nature. The body of an alien being would certainly constitute hard evidence.

Responding to this argument, believers point out that the hard evidence skeptics insist on may well exist but not be available to the public because of efforts by the air force and/or other government agencies to keep it hidden and highly classified. And even if no such hard evidence has yet been found, say believers, that does not mean that the saucers do not have alien origins. After all the reports that can be explained as misinterpretations of natural phenomena are thrown out, at least several dozen truly mysterious cases remain. These, believers contend, cannot be explained as anything else but intelligently piloted craft.

Is Alien Intelligence Probable?

Behind the question of extraterrestrial origins for flying saucers lurks a more elementary question for believers and skeptics alike: Is the existence of sentient, or intelligent, alien life even probable? People on both sides of the saucer debate accept that it is *possible*, since intelligent life did arise on earth and, therefore, one concrete example exists. However, this does not automatically prove that life, especially the sentient variety, has arisen elsewhere. What if the appearance of life on earth was a freak occurrence, highly unlikely to be repeated anywhere else in the universe? The important question, then, is not whether intelligent life *can* arise, for it obviously can, but rather, whether such life is common or rare.

The logical starting point in attempting to answer this question is the earth itself, or more precisely, the primordial, or early and primitive, earth. By examining how life began on earth, scientists seek clues about the possible formation of life on other planets. Because they cannot go back and witness firsthand what happened, researchers try to reproduce the conditions of the primordial earth. The goal is to see whether under laboratory conditions organic, or living, particles directly develop somehow from inorganic, or nonliving, ones. The classic experiment of this kind was performed in 1953 by Stanley Miller, a graduate student at the University of Chicago, and his professor, Dr. Harold Urey. They suspected that the beginnings of life may have been ignited by the action of lightning, radiation, and other forms of energy on inorganic substances in the earth's early oceans and soil. According to Carl Sagan, using a lab flask to contain the experiment, the men

> prepared a mixture of methane, ammonia, water, and hydrogen as a simulated primitive atmosphere. . . . High energy electrons were passed between two electrodes through the simulated primitive atmosphere. Such a flow of electrons is an adequate lightning simulation. . . . After a week of sparking, the liquid [in the flask] turned a deep brown. Clearly, new molecules were being produced from methane, ammonia, water, and hydrogen. But which ones? Were they organic?

It turned out that the new molecules were indeed organic, and among the substances identified were five amino acids which are used to make proteins, the building blocks of living cells and tissues. In the years that followed, other researchers repeated the

Scientist Stanley Miller at work in his lab in the 1950s. His experiments showed that the basic building blocks of life can, under the right conditions, spring up spontaneously from non-living materials.

Miller-Urey experiment and in every case the results were similar. The obvious conclusion seemed to be that the formation of the basic substances needed for life is a fairly easy process. "If this could be done in small volumes over very short periods of time," Isaac Asimov asked, "what could have been done in an entire ocean over a period of many millions of years?" And, broadening the question, what might have happened in the oceans on alien worlds? The fact is that hydrogen and the other materials present on the primordial earth are among the most plentiful in the universe. Therefore, the chances of Earth-like planets producing some kind of basic, primitive life seem high. In fact, as science writers Terence Dickinson and Adolf Schaller point out in their book, *Extraterrestrials: A Field Guide for Earthlings*, "If only one star in a billion is parent to a planet with life, then at least one trillion planets in the universe harbor living matter."

Immense Distances

But it is a long way from primitive life-forms battling to survive on alien planets to sentient beings leaving those planets and visiting the earth. Most scientists believe that even if the formation of elementary life is fairly common, the development of intelligent life-forms may be exceedingly rare. The evolution of lower life-forms into higher ones is a long and tortuous process absorbing billions of years and involving millions of trillions of random events. It is possible that only a few scattered planets succeed in producing sentient beings.

Of these beings, some may not develop the technology needed for space travel or, if they do, they may have moral or political reasons for refraining from such an endeavor. It may be, as Dickinson and Schaller suggest, that "We are the most advanced civilization in our sector of the universe; therefore, *we* have to find *them*." Or, as Asimov and numerous other skeptics have suggested, many such beings might use their advanced technology to destroy themselves before they develop the capacity to leave their own solar systems. After all, the specters of nuclear and biological warfare even now hang over humanity. No one can say for sure that the human race, the only sentient race that we know for certain to exist, will survive long enough to send piloted craft to other solar systems.

Scientists and other saucer skeptics argue further that even if a few intelligent races are engaged in space travel, the chances of their visiting the earth are slim. This is because of the vast distances that separate individual star systems. Even Alpha

A time-lapse exposure of the Milky Way, the galaxy in which our sun and earth reside. The trail of a communications satellite appears in the foreground.

Centauri, the closest star (excluding the sun), is 26 trillion miles away. To make such huge distances easier to visualize, scientists use a measure of distance called the light-year, or the distance that light, at a velocity of 186,000 miles per second, travels in a year. Thus, Alpha Centauri is about 4.3 light-years from earth. And the Milky Way, the vast spinning wheel of billions of stars in which the earth and its sun reside, is some 100,000 light-years in diameter.

To bridge these immense distances, say skeptics, space travelers would have to endure hundreds or thousands of years of flight time, expending vast amounts of energy. Consider visitors from a planet circling Alpha Centauri, for instance. Even traveling at forty times the velocity of the fastest spacecraft yet devised by humans, these visitors would require a thousand years to reach the earth. Philip Klass has allowed for advanced technologies capable of producing even higher speeds. "At a speed of *67 million miles per hour*," he says, "a single trip to earth [from Alpha Centauri] and back home would require almost a *century* to accomplish."

All other stars, of course, are much farther away than Alpha Centauri. According to Sagan, in his book *Intelligent Life in the Universe*, even if there are as many as fifty thousand civilizations more advanced than our own in the galaxy, they will be separated from one another by about a thousand light-years. So, the skeptics argue, long-range space travel, even for advanced beings, may not be very practical. Klass sums it up, saying that a visitation of earth by aliens "is not likely to happen, even once, simply because of the gigantic distance that separates our planet from all possible sources of intelligent life."

Gateways to Space and Time?

Believers agree with the skeptics that the immense galactic distances and the limitations they place on space travel are daunting. But many believers argue that these limitations are not impossible to overcome and suggest that some alien races may have found ways to do so. For example, some beings may have very long natural life spans or may have discovered the means of achieving practical immortality. Even now, say believers, human scientists are attempting to find ways of extending people's lives. Aliens thousands or even millions of years ahead of us in technical and medical knowledge may live long enough to take long interstellar trips in their stride.

Or perhaps the aliens traverse the galaxy in huge "space arks." These would be manufactured vehicles or maybe hollowed-out asteroids equipped with all the essentials for supporting a large colony. Science fiction writers often call these "generation ships" because many generations would live and die on them knowing full well that they would never see their native worlds again. Once such a mother ship reached an inhabited solar system like our own, it might go into orbit and then send out smaller, exploratory craft to study the various planets.

"Our galaxy is some 10,000 million years old and contains something on the order of 100,000 million stars. It is hard to believe that in all this myriad host of suns and throughout all these countless millennia not one race has developed without achieving a degree of practical interstellar [spaceflight] capability."

British astronomer John W. Macvey, *Interstellar Travel: Past, Present, and Future*

"Might it be, then, that civilizations are self-limiting, and that the reason civilizations elsewhere have not made themselves known to us is that they don't endure long enough to be heard from?"

Isaac Asimov, *Extraterrestrial Civilizations*

Another argument believers frequently use is the suggestion that Einstein was wrong—that it is in fact possible to exceed the speed of light. According to this view, alien physicists and engineers may have found ways to propel space vehicles faster than 186,000 miles per second. One such way that even many scientists concede is theoretically possible is by utilizing space "warps" or "wormholes," bizarre gateways that might lead to "hyperspace," a region of space outside the known universe. As Richard Williams explains:

> The central idea is that holes exist within our space-time continuum [visible, measurable universe] through which matter can enter or exit from hyperspace. A craft may "drop out" of space at one point and reappear at another position thousands, or even millions of light-years away. For this to be possible, a fourth dimension must exist through which a spacecraft can take shortcuts inaccessible in a three-dimensional world.

Black holes, extremely dense entities with gravity forces so strong that even light cannot escape, are often cited as possible locations of space warps leading into hyperspace.

Some believers eliminate the problem of galactic distances altogether by suggesting that the "pilots" of flying saucers are *not* inhabitants of other planets at all. For example, one theory, put forward in the 1960s by ufologist Alan Greenfield, suggests that the visitors might come from "alternate dimensions." The concept of such dimensions is somewhat similar to that of hyperspace. But whereas hyperspace is seen as a formless void, other dimensions are, hypothetically, other material universes like, but hidden from, our own. According to this idea, the visitors materialize on earth at special and presumably invisible points where their dimension intersects with ours.

Another theory that periodically crops up in the saucer literature proposes that the saucers are vehicles from humanity's own distant future. In this scenario, our descendants have discovered the means of time travel and are either studying us or using our genes and hormones to revitalize the aging, decaying human race. Believers who ascribe to this theory point out that it provides a motive for saucer abductions and also explains how the beings would be able to crossbreed with humans.

Earthly Explanations

Skeptics generally respond to such theories with the same argument they use against the idea that the saucers are alien craft, namely that no hard evidence exists to support them. Menzel, Klass, Vallée, and other noted skeptics have spent much of their time trying to show how saucer sightings and experiences can be explained in terms of documented physical phenomena. If the saucers can be accounted for in these ways, say the skeptics, there is no need to resort to more exotic theories involving hyperspace, time travel, and the like. Carl Sagan provides a list, much like those cited by Klass and other skeptics, of natural phenomena that have been mistaken for flying saucers:

> unconventional aircraft; aircraft under uncommon weather conditions; balloons; artificial earth satellites; flocks of birds; reflections of searchlights or headlights off clouds; reflection of sunlight from shiny surfaces . . . optical mirages and . . . lenticular cloud formations; ball lightning; sun dogs [reflections of sunlight on ice crystals]; meteors . . . planets, especially Venus; bright stars; and the Aurora Borealis [the so-called northern lights].

Some of the most common such mistakes, say skeptics, have involved clouds. British astronomer John W. Macvey witnessed a striking example on a flight from Britain to Florida in 1971:

Lenticular clouds, photographed over Mt. Shasta, California. Such clouds can easily be mistaken for solid, disk-shaped objects.

From the top of one . . . cloud, driven no doubt by the prevailing wind at that altitude, there separated five small tufts of cloud each of which at once adopted a nearly circular configuration [shape] and proceeded on its own in line ahead. The "leader". . . was the largest. Once all were clear of the parent cloud they assumed an almost textbook "flying saucer" formation—"mother ship" and four attendant "scouts."

Another kind of cloud phenomenon commonly mistaken for flying craft are "noctilucent" clouds. These consist of patches of dust particles that are swept along by winds at high altitudes and at very high speeds. The patches, seen only at night, reflect glints of sunlight or moonlight back to viewers on the ground, giving the impression of spherical, moving aircraft.

Mock suns, or "sun dogs," basically bright reflections of sunlight from atmospheric ice crystals, sometimes provide similar such impressions of flying craft. A well-known case of a mock sun occurred off the coast of England in 1926. "The image," reports scientist William R. Corliss in his book *Handbook of Unusual Natural Phenomena*, "had the appearance of the true sun [a round, bright disk] shining through denser layers of cloud."

Other unusual but explainable phenomena frequently mistaken for saucers include swamp gas and ball lightning. Some visible outbursts of swamp gas, often referred to as "will-o'-the-wisps," are softly glowing gas bubbles generated by decaying vegetable matter in swamps. The luminous bubbles have been known to move along both vertically and horizontally and can appear to be solid objects. Ball lightning is a mysterious form of electricity that appears in spheres, rods, spiked balls, and other odd shapes. It can remain visible for extended periods, and, writes Corliss, "may glide silently and disinterestedly past

This drawing depicts two mock suns, or "sun dogs," caused by sunlight reflecting off ice crystals in the upper atmosphere.

an observer or it may inquisitively explore a room as if directed by intelligence."

Exceptions to the Rule

One of the strongest rebuttals of the idea that all saucer sightings can be explained away as occurrences of natural phenomena came from the late J. Allen Hynek. As a trained scientist who kept a completely open mind when investigating flying saucers, Hynek, unlike most of his scientific colleagues, in a sense bridged the gap between skeptics and believers. He agreed that many, if not most, of the saucer reports were based on encounters with known earthly phenomena. However, after numerous and thorough investigations, he firmly held that a small number of cases could not be so explained and therefore remained "unknowns."

Hynek suggested that flying saucers might constitute yet another rare but very real phenomenon, only in this case one that could not be explained in earthly terms. As with other very rare phenomena,

An artist's depiction of the mysterious glowing phenomenon that can be caused by swamp gas.

Dr. Allen Hynek (right), who, during his many years of studying the flying saucer phenomenon, always kept an open mind.

he wrote, strong evidence explaining the saucers is lacking because of the great difficulty of collecting data about these objects. To get such data, researchers must, as in cases like ball lightning and meteorites, "rely on the fortuitous [lucky] observations of the layman." But the small portion of unexplainable data that *is* collected may have vital and momentous significance. "The history of science," Hynek declared, "has shown that it is the things that *don't* fit, the apparent exceptions to the rule, that signal potential breakthroughs in our concept of the world about us."

The breakthrough that Hynek wanted so much to witness was the conclusive documentation of flying saucers as extraterrestrial craft. He did not live to see such proof. But those few "things that don't fit," the "unknowns" he spent his adult life investigating, continue to be reported and recorded. And despite the great distances to the stars and the frequent misinterpretations of exotic earthly phenomena, the skeptics have yet satisfactorily to explain these unknowns.

Epilogue

They Will Keep Watching the Skies

The debate that began in 1947 after Kenneth Arnold claimed to have seen nine silvery disks zooming by Mt. Rainier continues. On one side loom formidable skeptics, armed with scientific principles, logical arguments, and persistent doubts. Saucer debunker Philip Klass neatly summed up the skeptical viewpoint in 1974 by labeling flying saucers a myth:

> The myth of extraterrestrial visitors will persist . . . if only because there are so many natural and man-made "UFOs" to be seen, and because so many people *want* to believe.

On the other side of the debate stand stalwart believers, intrigued by unexplained phenomena and convinced that conventional science has not provided satisfactory answers for some of these unusual occurrences. The believers contend that most scientists have dismissed the saucer phenomenon out of hand without according it sufficient serious analysis. "The UFO evidence has not been properly presented in the Court of Science," J. Allen Hynek remarked in 1975. Hynek made an impassioned plea "for the proper scientific study" of flying saucers. "When the nature of the UFO controversy is understood," he said, "a meaningful start can be made on

a truly scientific study of the subject, which can then be approached as scientific subjects should be approached—without prejudice or emotional bias."

After a half century of controversy, as the twenty-first century begins, the flying saucer mystery remains unsolved and the debate about that mystery rages on. Conclusive evidence that will satisfy all the skeptics may suddenly appear tomorrow, next month, or next year. Or centuries may pass before proof arrives, if, in fact, it ever does. But however long it takes, it is unlikely that believers will give up their quest for that evidence. They will remain vigilant, and they will keep watching the skies.

A 1981 photo purporting to show a flying saucer speeding over Vancouver, British Columbia. The true nature of such objects remains both a mystery and a matter of debate.

For Further Exploration

George C. Andrews, *Extra-Terrestrials Among Us*. St. Paul, MN: Llewellyn Publications, 1987.

Michael Arvey, *UFOs: Opposing Viewpoints*. San Diego, CA: Greenhaven Press, 1989.

Jim Collins, *Unidentified Flying Objects*. Milwaukee, WI: Raintree Children's Books, 1977.

John A. Keel, *Strange Creatures from Time and Space*. Greenwich, CT: Fawcett, 1970.

Don Nardo, *Gravity: The Universal Force*. San Diego, CA: Lucent Books, 1990.

Carl Sagan, *Cosmos*. New York: Random House, 1980.

Carl Sagan and Thorton Page, eds., *UFOs: A Scientific Debate*. New York: Norton, 1974.

Ivan T. Sanderson, *Uninvited Visitors*. New York: Cowles, 1967.

Ron Story, *The Space-Gods Revealed: A Close Look at the Theories of Erich von Daniken*. New York: Harper & Row, 1976.

Walter Sullivan, *We Are Not Alone*. New York: McGraw-Hill, 1964.

Jean-Pierre Verdet, *The Sky: Mystery, Magic, and Myth*. New York: Harry N. Abrams, 1992.

Note: The author also highly recommends the following well-written and absorbing science fiction works, which deal with human contact with alien technology and civilizations:

Isaac Asimov, *The Gods Themselves*. New York: Fawcett-Crest, 1972.

Isaac Asimov et al., eds., *Flying Saucers* (collection of short stories). New York: Fawcett-Crest, 1982.

Greg Bear, *The Forge of God*. New York: Tom Doherty, 1987.

Arthur C. Clark, *Childhood's End*. New York: Ballantine Books, 1953.

———, *2001, A Space Odyssey*. New York: New American Library, 1968.

———, *2010, Odyssey Two*. New York: Ballantine Books, 1982.

Fred Hoyle, *The Black Cloud*. New York: New American Library, 1957.

Donald Moffitt, *The Genesis Quest*. New York: Ballantine Books, 1986.

Larry Niven and Jerry Pournelle, *Footfall*. New York: Ballantine Books, 1985.

———, *The Mote in God's Eye*. New York: Pocket Books, 1974.

Carl Sagan, *Contact*. New York: Simon & Schuster, 1985.

Whitley Strieber, *Majestic*. New York: G. P. Putnam's Sons, 1989.

H. G. Wells, *The War of the Worlds*. First published in 1898; many available editions.

John Wyndham, *Chocky*. New York: Ballantine Books, 1968.

Jim Wynorski, ed., *They Came from Outer Space* (12 classic short stories). Garden City, NY: Doubleday, 1980.

Works Consulted

George Adamski, *Inside the Space Ships*. New York: Abelard-Schuman, 1955.

Kenneth Arnold and Ray Palmer, *The Coming of the Saucers*. Privately printed. Boise, ID: 1952.

Isaac Asimov, *A Choice of Catastrophes*. New York: Simon & Schuster, 1979.

———, *Extraterrestrial Civilizations*. New York: Crown, 1979.

Howard Blum, *Out There: The Government's Secret Quest for Extraterrestrials*. New York: Simon & Schuster, 1990.

Ben Bova and Byron Preiss, eds., *First Contact*. New York: Penguin Books, 1990.

Maurice Chatelaine, *Our Ancestors Came from Outer Space*. Garden City, NY: Doubleday, 1978.

William R. Corliss, *Handbook of Unusual Natural Phenomena: Eyewitness Accounts of Nature's Greatest Mysteries*. New York: Arlington House, 1986.

Erich von Daniken, *Chariots of the Gods?* New York: Bantam Books, 1971.

———, *The Gold of the Gods*. New York: Bantam Books, 1972.

———, *Miracles of the Gods*. New York: Dell, 1974.

Terence Dickinson and Adolf Schaller, *Extraterrestrials: A Field Guide for Earthlings*. Camden, Ontario: Camden House, 1994.

Frank Edwards, *Flying Saucers—Serious Business*. New York: Lyle Stuart, 1966.

Randall Fitzgerald, *The Complete Book of Extraterrestrial Encounters*. New York: Collier Books, 1979.

John G. Fuller, *The Interrupted Journey*. New York: Dial Press, 1966.

J. Allen Hynek, *The UFO Experience: A Scientific Inquiry*. Chicago: Regnery, 1972.

David Michael Jacobs, *The UFO Controversy in America*. Bloomington: University of Indiana Press, 1975.

Donald E. Keyhoe, *Aliens from Space: The Real Story of Unidentified Flying Objects*. Garden City, NY: Doubleday, 1973.

———, *The Flying Saucer Conspiracy*. New York: Holt, Rinehart & Winston, 1955.

———, *The Flying Saucers Are Real*. New York: Fawcett, 1950.

———, *Flying Saucers: Top Secret*. New York: G. P. Putnam's Sons, 1960.

Philip J. Klass, *UFOs Explained*. New York: Random House, 1974.

John Lear, "Scientific Explanation for the UFOs?" *Saturday Review*, October 1, 1966.

John E. Mack, *Abductions: Human Encounters with Aliens*. New York: Charles Scribner's Sons, 1994.

John W. Macvey, *Interstellar Travel: Past, Present, and Future*. New York: Avon, 1977.

James M. McCampbell, *Ufology: A Major Breakthrough in the Scientific Understanding of Unidentified Flying Objects*. Millbrae, CA: Celestial Arts, 1976.

Robert B. McLaughlin, "How Scientists Tracked a Flying Saucer," *True*, March 1950.

Donald H. Menzel and Lyle B. Boyd, *The World of Flying Saucers: A Scientific Examination of a Major Myth of the Space Age*. Garden City, NY: Doubleday, 1963.

Donald H. Menzel and Ernest H. Taves, *The UFO Enigma*. Garden City, NY: Doubleday, 1977.

Curtis Peebles, *Watch the Skies!: A Chronicle of the Flying Saucer Myth*. Washington, DC: Smithsonian Institution Press, 1994.

Jenny Randles and Peter Warrington, *Science and the UFOs*. New York: Basil Blackwell, 1985.

Edward Ruppelt, *The Report on Unidentified Flying Objects*. Garden City, NY: Doubleday, 1956.

————, "What the Air Force Has Found Out About Flying Saucers," *True*, May 1954.

Carl Sagan, *Broca's Brain: Reflections on the Romance of Science*. New York: Ballantine Books, 1979.

————, *The Cosmic Connection*. New York: Dell, 1973.

————, "The Saucerian Cult," *Saturday Review*, August 6, 1966.

Carl Sagan and I. S. Shklovskii, *Intelligent Life in the Universe*. San Francisco: Holden-Day, 1966.

David R. Saunders and R. Roger Harkins, *UFOs? Yes!: Where the Condon Committee Went Wrong*. New York: World Publishing, 1968.

Brad Steiger, *Project Blue Book*. New York: Ballantine Books, 1976.

————, *Worlds Before Our Own*. New York: Berkeley, 1978.

Ronald D. Story, *Guardians of the Universe?* New York: St. Martin's Press, 1980.

Whitley Strieber, *Communion: A True Story*. New York: Avon, 1987.

Richard Williams, senior ed., *UFO: The Continuing Enigma*. Pleasantville, NY: Reader's Digest Association, 1991.

Index

About the Author

Don Nardo is an award-winning author whose more than sixty books cover a wide range of topics. In addition to this volume on the flying saucer phenomenon, his science-related studies include *Dinosaurs: Unearthing the Secrets of Ancient Beasts*, *Gravity: The Universal Force*, *Germs: Mysterious Microorganisms*, *Medical Diagnosis*, *Ozone*, *The Eternal Quest: Humanity's Ceaseless Efforts to Unlock the Secrets of the Universe*, and a biography of Charles Darwin. Mr. Nardo is also a trained historian and a screenwriter, having turned out over twenty-five history books and numerous screenplays and teleplays, including work for Warner Brothers and ABC Television. He lives with his wife Christine on Cape Cod, Massachusetts.

Picture Credits